The Broken Mirror

A Collection of Writings from Contemporary Poland

The Broken Mirror

A Collection of Writings from
Contemporary Poland

EDITED BY PAWEL MAYEWSKI

under the auspices of The East Europe Institute

INTRODUCTION BY LIONEL TRILLING

Random House
New York

Contents

Every man carries with him through life a mirror, as unique and impossible to get rid of as his shadow.

Most, perhaps all, our mirrors are inaccurate and uncomplimentary, though to varying degrees and in various ways. Some magnify, some diminish, others return lugubrious, comic, derisive, or terrifying images.

But the properties of our own particular mirror are not so important as we sometimes like to think. We shall be judged, not by the kind of mirror found on us, but by the use we have made of it, by our riposte to our reflection.

W. H. Auden

Editor's Note

The original purpose of this book was to acquaint the American reader with what some of the more prominent Polish intellectuals and writers have to say about the system in which they live now that the opportunity to say it has come their way. Recent happenings in Poland have been reported extensively in the press, but our knowledge of events is limited largely to facts recorded and commentaries supplied by experts; that is, to second-hand accounts. Although such information is valuable, the immediate impact of experience, its genuine meaning and tone, must be sought at the source—in the very words and gestures of those who are eye- and ear-deep in it. This, then, was the aim: to let the Poles describe the reality they live in themselves.

However, in selecting the material it began to seem as if this criterion was too narrow to do justice to the richness and intensity of present-day Polish writing. Reading the various reactions of Polish writers to their surroundings—their painful stocktaking of the recent past and their own participation in it—led me to believe that the matters they discussed had a significance and urgency which transcended national and political borders. Their self-questioning brought them to a consideration of wider and eternal issues—of man's relation to society, the problem of action or inaction, responsibility and guilt. In examining and re-examining these problems, they reflected the individual's attempt to grow in a reality that is never satisfying and not entirely of his own making; and though living in a place so distant and different from ours, what they said seemed of crucial importance not only for them, but also for us, in a world where the conflict of ideas and physical forces has made one man's business the business of other men.

As the book was being put together, it also became apparent that a selection of living experience does not allow unanimity of opinion. The works presented here express a variety of reactions, solutions and temperaments; what they share is sincerity of emotions—protest and agreement, rejection and acceptance, anger and love—in short, an overwhelming humanity. That these writings found their way into the Polish press suggests the peculiar propensity of the human mind to react when it can no longer bear the burden of its own passivity and artifice; and if this book demonstrates anything, it is the wisdom of the saying that even though a man walks a tightrope, he does not do so only to defy the law of gravity.

Introduction

This book must be thought of as an event. I do not say this as a manner of speaking, as critics sometimes do when they wish to suggest the intellectual or artistic importance of a work. This book is an event in the grosser and more usual sense in which we speak of an event in military or political history, such as a battle or an uprising. It comes to us laden with the past—it is the compendium and crux of many precedent events, most of them grim, all of them grave. And it is charged with the future, massive with what it may portend, and somber with undisclosed fate. For this is an event that has yet to reach its conclusion; its issue, which is of an ultimate importance, has not yet been decided.

The writers whose work is brought together in this volume are all Poles. Most of them are young or youngish. All of them are, or have been, Communists, or in active sympathy with the Communist Party. But what constitutes the most significant element of their homogeneity is that, in a Communist state, their relation to Communism being what it is, they fulfill the function which we have come to think of as virtually definitive of the ideal conception of the intellectual: they assert an intense critical preoccupation with the relationship that should properly exist between society and intellect. They conceive this right relation to be one in which the intellect is free, in which the Reason of State does not provide the excuse for the State to limit and control the activity of mind. The terms in which they express this idea are not in the least recondite, but, on the contrary, very simple and easy to recognize—they are the terms of the long tradition of humanism which holds that freedom of thought is a necessary condition for the acquiring of knowledge and for seeking truth, and also a good in itself.

At this point we must deal with the fact that these intellectuals—and I should add, these remarkably gifted intellectuals—were able for a time to express their ideas about society, and their hopes for it, through the ideology of Communism. By 1944, when Poland became a Communist state, there can have been no doubt about the nature of Communism as it had been established in Russia. No intelligent person could have been ignorant of the conditions of life in the Soviet Union; no intellectual could have been under any illusion about the conditions of the cultural life. What is more, the Russian behavior to Poland before and during and after the war gave clear and overwhelming evidence of the nature of the Communist morality. Nothing could have been more calculatedly ruthless than the Soviet intentions toward Poland. They involved not only a large territorial depredation but the eventual control of the whole nation through the establishment of a Communist regime. The latter enterprise was carried out by the systematic destruction of those elements—that is to say, of those people—whose political views were not likely to lead them to cooperate with the Communist government that was being contrived in Moscow. It was politics by decimation, and certain episodes of its practice perhaps still stick in the ever-shortening memory of modern man: the deportation of 1,500,000 Poles to Russia; the massacre of the 10,000 Polish officers in the Katyn forest; the refusal of Russian airfields to the Allied flyers who stood ready to help the people of Warsaw in their desperate uprising against the Germans and the immobility of the Russian army outside the city until a sufficient number of the insurgents should have been killed.

There were the facts, all clear to the view, beyond any possibility of being unknown. Yet even the traditional strong, overt feeling for their nation which still marks Polish intellectuals did not deter many of them from embracing Communism, the ideology of their nation's traditional enemy.

There were the facts, all clear to the view. But it is characteristic of a well-developed ideology that it can diminish or destroy the primitive potency of fact. This is especially true when an ideology embodies, as Communism does, the idea of "history," of process and progress—the fact of today, let alone of yesterday, becomes of no account before the adjustment and recompense that the future will bring. Sometimes, as we know, it is possible for the Communist ideology to make this effect even on the minds of people who live in an established and secure society. How much more readily will it make this effect on the minds of people whose nation has been overrun, whose economy has been destroyed, whose society has been shattered. One could not have a more moving account of what it means to exist under circumstances of this kind than Tadeusz Rozewicz's story in this volume, "The New Philosophical School." All that is left to people thus situated is the hope of restored community with their fellow men. That, and some idea of the future. More often than not the idea of the future is supplied to them by Communism —all over the world the intellectuals of disadvantaged countries can find no other idea of the future to be of equal power. Democracy, contrary to the fond expectations which Americans for a time entertained, is not for them an available idea. Even if they accept at face value and with the best will in the world the virtues we claim for democracy, when they think of democracy as a system of social organization, they conceive it to be ineluctably bound up, if not with capitalism, which almost inevitably they reject, then with an economic development far beyond any they can envisage for themselves in the near future. To such people the very rigors of Communism may well appear to lend the color of truth to the ideology. The system is validated by the hardship it entails. Desperate people do not easily imagine felicity—they will feel that what is appropriate to their hope is not security or comfort but some way of bringing to an end the humiliation of being passive under deprivation and suffering. They seek some consistent principle of action and they are the more reassured if the consistency is systematic and rigorous.

Eventually, however, the Polish intellectuals understood that Communism entailed not only the hardship they may well have envisaged but also a moral corruption which they had not permitted themselves to foresee. The writers whose work we read in this volume make their affirmations of freedom of mind in indignation and bitterness at the restraints that were put upon their minds, but also in disgust at what they were willing to believe, in revulsion from what they consented to say.

The intellectual life of Poland under Communism never matched the monolithic conformity of the intellectual life of Russia. The best known representation of Communist Poland is Czeslaw Milosz's *The Captive Mind*; this is a work to be admired on several scores, but more than one trustworthy observer has said that it goes beyond the facts in representing the Polish intellectuals as having wholly and happily capitulated to the Communist mystique. There was, of course, quite a considerable adherence to Communism on the basis of genuine conviction. But opportunism would seem to explain the adherence of some people, as no doubt prudence explains the consent of many more. The Catholic Church was indeed hard pressed by the government and quite effectually limited and controlled. But with the population almost entirely Catholic and inclined to be devout, the Church could not be liquidated and it served as a countervailing force. In its cultural life Poland had always been of the West; the regime undertook to orient the nation toward Russia and fostered hostility to Western, and especially to American, culture. It was a policy that met with no permanent success; the art and ideas of the West continued to engage the Poles and served to support a growing antagonism to Russia, which eventually found expression in politics, even in the Party itself.

In short, the Polish situation was of a kind in which it was possible for the intellectual life to survive. It had at least enough looseness to allow individual thinkers and writers to imagine that movement and change were not beyond hope, that there might be some point in asking questions about the State and about themselves. We may say that it was a situation that at least licensed the awareness of boredom and disgust, from which springs much of the energy of the intellectual and artistic life.

But the correction of Milosz's picture must not lead us to minimize the harshness which did actually prevail in the intellectual life of Poland. How very bad were the conditions of that life is abundantly attested to in the present volume. Pawel Hertz calls his reminiscences of the "sad years" between 1949 and 1953 "Recollections from the House of the Dead." The House of the Dead is his name for the offices of the Writers' Union. I have been told that there were no executions in punishment of cultural deviations — the Dead to whom Hertz refers are only spiritually deceased. But they were brought to their condition by coercion, even if that fell short of the threat of the penalty of actual death. Hertz leaves us in no doubt about this: "The atmosphere of gloom, evoked by drilling writers ceaselessly, admonishing them, using open threats, constantly identifying any non-conformity in thinking with hostility, qualifying opposition in cultural and theoretical matters by paragraphs of the criminal code — all this to the accompaniment of an increasing number of political trials and a mounting wave of arrests, silenced the literary group. The paradoxical situation arose in which ardent speakers at rallies would inveigh against their own interpretations of the ideas of their silent opponents." Inevitably, as Hertz goes on to say, "literature lost its moral and intellectual prestige and the writer lost the confidence of his own society."

In his striking play about the death of Socrates, "The Philosophers' Den," Zbigniew Herbert speaks of men who "have mastered the art of acquiescence." This is not a silent art. It is the art of speaking out loud and clear in the way one is expected to speak. And in order to speak as one is expected to, it is not enough to say the right things in the most orthodox way possible; one must make whatever one says a negation of that critical, dialectical, ironic (I use the words in the senses appropriate to Socrates) movement of mind which is the very essence of the intellectual life. To the truly acquiescent man all things must be as obvious, and as meaningless, as Socrates himself is to the Keeper of the jail.

> . . . It's a simple matter really. Socrates was of proletarian origin. His father tried to make a living from his workshop, but he didn't get on too well. Competition, huge factories, big manufacturers—you understand. Socrates had to go out on the streets and earn his living by talking — so he became a philosopher because of economic conditions.
>
> —Who made a martyr of him?
>
> He did himself—or to be more exact, it was the result of his inability to understand the mechanism of history. As a proletarian, he ought to have become a people's tribune, an agitator. His platform was prepared for him: to fight, on the one hand against the reactionary upper bourgeoisie, and on the other, to seek for close contact with the progressive lower bourgeoisie. Simple, eh? But he preferred aristocracy and its precious disputes—about what is good and what is evil, about abstract justice from the moon. So he fell from the moon straight into jail. Thus one pays for betraying one's class. Bye, bye. Fight mosquitoes and idealism.

The indignation and bitterness and the boredom and disgust eventually found their expression. The present volume exemplifies the intensity of the affirmations of intellectual liberty that were made by the Polish intellectuals after the early months of 1956. And to a reader with any imagination of the way in which a cultural tendency accelerates, it will suggest how numerous such affirmations are. Few events of our time are so stirring as this large and dramatic repudiation of the Stalinist hegemony in culture. As it is exemplified in this volume, it is virtually unequivocal. There is but one instance of a writer finding it in his heart to say a word in apology for the old order. This occurs in Kazimierz Brandys's *nouvelle*, "The Defense of Granada," a work which is as accomplished as it is informative. The occasion is the last speech of Doctor Faul, the all-powerful Stalinist pundit who has been the puppet-master and Gray Eminence of the life of art, a man—or a figure—hated and feared by all. When the great change has come, he is permitted to surround himself with an aura of high dialectical-materialistic pathos as he speaks of the historical inevitability of his role, of the pain it had cost him to discharge his duty to the Revolution. But no other writer than Brandys gives any sign of a desire to save the face of Stalinism and the past. Nor does any other writer make use of the mode of thought which Brandys employs in tribute, as it were, to a former self. One of the striking things about this volume is the frank directness of the writers as they deal with past events to which they had been committed, and the happiness with which they exercise their common sense and their plain human judgment; the air they breathe is the bright air of reason and intention, not the miasma of historical necessity.

It is scarcely possible that anyone will read this book without feeling the impulse to be heartened for the future. The human mind, we are impelled to say, cannot be prevented forever from asserting its own nature and its own best needs.

It is a true thing to say, but if we say it, we must also say that the needs of the human mind are still very much at odds with the needs of most powerful forces.

If we speak of the future, we must speak with circumspec-

7

tion. We must take into account the fact that the assertion of freedom in Poland was not wholly autonomous. In saying this, I do not mean to question the autonomy of the intellectuals' desire for freedom. And certainly I do not mean to question the autonomy of their thought as they developed it under adverse conditions and as they now express it. But the freedom which they now claim for themselves was, up to a point, *permitted*. It was one of the consequences of the "thaw," as it is called, that took place in Russia after the death of Stalin. I am aware that there were notable demonstrations of Polish intellectual independence before the thaw, but the full outburst was subsequent to it. Granted that the behavior of the Poles went beyond the point of permission, that the waters flowed more freely than had perhaps been anticipated by those who decreed that the ice should melt, that even the Communist Party of Poland asserted an independence that had not been bargained for by the Russian Party—it is still true that the situation in Poland followed upon a decision of the Russian Party.

Only one writer in the present volume observes this. In his "Notes for a Biography," Wiktor Woroszylski remarks that a colleague had expressed himself as being outraged because the thaw had not been initiated by the artists themselves. To this Woroszylski replies: "I personally do not feel humiliated that, thanks to the decisive moves of the leadership of the Communist Party of the Soviet Union, and of our own Party, I acquired the vision I had lacked before, so essential for resolving my doubts and unrest."

Taken out of its context, this has an ominous sound, which does not, however, do justice to its author. For Woroszylski goes on to qualify his acceptance of Party direction— he speaks of being gratified by the fact that the artists and intellectuals had entered the new era "not as docile agents and barometer-watchers, but as deeply committed participants." I understand him to be saying by this that he finds it possible to receive his "vision" from the Party because the Party decision was made in response to the desires of the artists and intellectuals, that he believes the thaw to be indicative of the Party's intention to democratize itself.

So far as Poland goes, this may be a reasonable belief. Even though I have in memory the disturbing suppression of *Po Prostu*, I should not want to close my mind to the possibility that the Communist Party of Poland is, or will become, a Communist Party of a different kind from that of Russia, and that it is responsive to the actual wishes of the Polish people. I cannot presume to say what the political wishes of the Polish people are, but I think there is little doubt about what the intellectuals want—a humane and humanistic socialism. In his essay in the present volume, Leszek Kolakowski moves gently and circumspectly as he undertakes to distinguish the permanent from the transitory aspects of Marxism, but the results of his discrimination are radical: by the transitory aspects of Marxism he means Stalinism, which he quite rejects; by the permanent aspects of Marxism he means a kind of pragmatism or instrumentalism. Jan Strzelecki in his "Notes: 1950-1953" goes somewhat further than Kolakowski. Basing himself on assumptions that are flagrantly humanistic, he questions in an ironic and most cogent way the very psychology of the revolutionary and dismisses the creed upon which the revolutionary culture has existed for some three decades. If this is to be the direction of Polish thought, and if the ideas of Polish writers are going to make their way into politics and find eventual expression in the policies of a democratized Party, then indeed it will be possible for a considerable measure of freedom to be established in Poland under national Communism.

But is the question of Polish freedom to be answered in Poland? I think not—I think it is to be answered in Russia. Woroszylski, in proposing the idea that the thaw is an aspect of the democratization of the Party, means the Russian as well as the Polish Party. There will be not a few in the West to share his belief. Of these I am not one. I am sure that in the

Soviet Union there are many people who are as eager for intellectual freedom as were the intellectuals of Poland. I am sure that the Party will not grant it to them. Even a little freedom is a dangerous thing—those who have a little never fail to want a great deal more. And intellectual freedom can produce nothing that the Soviet Union, at this moment of its history, can be supposed to find use for—unless it can also be supposed that the Soviet Union intends now to bring to an end its efforts to extend its power. A class of free Russian intellectuals would in all likelihood deal with Marxism in a way not very different from the way in which Polish intellectuals are dealing with it. That is to say, they would demonstrate the emptiness and inhumanity of Stalinist Marxism. Russia may not at the moment wish to cherish anything that bears Stalin's name—although who can tell what will be cherished a few months hence?—but Stalinist Marxism, under whatever name, is essential to Russia. You do not undertake to convert or subvert or conquer the world with a program of pragmatism or instrumentalism. Humanism does not encourage the iron single-mindedness that is needed for domination. For this only Stalinist Marxism will serve.

No, I cannot imagine that freedom will come to the Russian intellectuals in the near future. And if it does not, and if it does remain to the Polish intellectuals, and if the tenor of their thought continues to be as I have described it, and if their ideas actually do have a decisive influence in the political life of the nation, then Poland will not be what the Soviet Party intended it should be, an instrument of the Soviet Union, and indeed scarcely even an appropriate ally. If the Soviet Union consents to be balked of its purpose, Polish freedom may survive and develop; if not, not.

Does it need to be said that the danger in which the Polish intellectuals stand makes their affirmation of freedom the more splendid?

New York, January 1958

10

Tadeusz Rozewicz

The New Philosophical School

(a postwar story)

It was the end of October, or perhaps the end of November, 1945.

I knocked at the white door. Behind it, I heard the murmuring and grunting of a large game animal. I walked into the room of a philosopher. He was the most distinguished contemporary Polish philosopher—Husserl's student, if I'm not mistaken.

I had signed up at the university in the fall. The professor lectured on "an introduction to the theory of knowledge." I was burning with a strange ambition: to attend the seminar lectures without having to go through all the preparatory courses of study. Why do I call my ambition strange? Because at that time I was convinced men were a herd of two-footed animals, crazed with fear. The herd (to which I belonged), terrified by fire and inspired by the scent of blood, still was able to hunt for food, to digest it and to fornicate.

But I will not talk about all that now.

I nodded to the professor, explained to him briefly who I

was and what I was doing in his office, and asked to be accepted in his class. He smiled. In a warm, hoarse voice he told me that I first had to go through the pre-seminar course. I made a face. He looked at me more closely and said, "Oh well, you see . . . what philosophers do you know? What have you read? . . . Please tell me."

Frantically, I began to search the past.

I liked his face and the structure of his head. It was a precision machine, constructed fifty years ago or thereabouts in the famous German academies of higher learning. It worked well—despite war damage. A striking, unusual phenomenon. Only sometimes, during his lectures, he stood silently at the window, thinking. Outside, he could see a fragment of wall and the November sky.

I stood before him in my engineering corps boots, remnants of my "forest days," and tried to recall the names of various philosophers.

"I have read Socrates," I said laconically and fell silent. The professor smiled and tilted his head. "Or, to be exact, not Socrates but Plato," I corrected myself. "I have read Plato, Nietzsche. . . ." He smiled again. "I have also read Bergson's *Creative Evolution*," I added with pride. He seemed to be waiting for something. . . . Slowly, the names of other philosophers, heard during my high school days, came back. The names of "philosophers" and the names of friends with whom I had discussed the meaning of life, the purpose of life, God.

"I have also read Spencer and Draper."

I mentioned these two names with some uncertainty because I no longer remembered what I had read by them. I remembered only that I had read something by one of them —with Zbyszek. In the park, a year before the war broke out. It was a book, or rather a brochure, in a green cover. I had forgotten its title or, for that matter, its contents. It was, after all, quite possible that someone altogether different had written the book. I remembered only that one chapter discussed Catholic dogma; the author asked sarcastically whether anyone "ever had seen the finger of the Holy Ghost." I remembered that part about "the finger" though I no longer had any idea what it was all about. I gave up and cut short my reminiscences. After a brief silence I mentioned another name: Freud. The professor looked up, as if interested. This for some reason reminded me of a joke about a dream in which the dreamer opened the bottom drawer of his wardrobe and emptied himself into it; this was supposed to signify his desire, suppressed in childhood, to have sexual intercourse with his nurse. But the whole thing was merely a joke. Though, as far as the leg was concerned, I was certain that I had read something about its role in sexual life, probably in one of Freud's books. The author's deductions seemed to us so comical that we, Zbyszek and I, learned them by heart. I can recite the pertinent fragments even now: ". . . the foot is an eternal sexual symbol in all myths. Consequently, a boot or a shoe is the symbol of the female sexual organ. Thus in fetishistic forms of perversion only a dirty and foul-smelling foot is a sexual object. . . . The foot is thus conceived of as the female's sexual organ whose absence is felt strongly by children. . . ." Obviously, we ignored certain logical parts in the deductions so that, as a result, we had such an idiotic and ridiculous impression of the whole thing that we simply burst out laughing.

Leaning toward me, the professor seemed to be waiting for other names. I had already mentioned all the names I knew. I finished with a word about Schopenhauer's pessimism. As from darkness, from a huge, deep well, there arose one more name. But I did not mention it to the professor. It had a strange, foreign sound and I had not come across it since childhood. "Mulfort." That was the name of the mysterious philosopher. I had never read anything by Mulfort myself, simply because I could not read or write at the time, but he was read to me by an old man who was married to a woman with black, burning eyes. Unfortunately, I knew very little about Mulfort. I no longer remembered whether he wrote about hypnotism or hygiene; it may very well be that he wrote about hippopotami or perhaps even about hashish. He probably was an Englishman.

His was the last name I mentioned, or rather remembered. Anyway, I always seemed to confuse his name with that of "mouflon." But then I did not even know what a "mouflon" looked like. Where did that animal live and what did he feed on? I knew, however, with some degree of certainty, that he had turned-up horns and long, woolly hair. It was also possible that he gave milk, though this may have been pure assumption on my part. About Mulfort himself I knew absolutely nothing.

I had also heard a few things about Kant, but always in connection with jokes. Was it Kant who said, "The starry sky above me and the moral law within me"? I waited to hear what the professor had to say.

His eyes burned for a while and then the fire in them died. He was tired, though he must have been enjoying himself. Or was he perhaps tired and astonished?

"You fought with a weapon in your hand while we were saving human thought. You fought in the forest, we . . . wherever it was possible. I will be happy to accept you in my class. We are now reading Hume's *Treatise on Human Nature*." He shook hands with me. I bowed and left the room.

Later, I went to the university restaurant. I waited behind the chair of another student until he finished his meal. All of the students ate very quickly because other, equally hungry students, were waiting with spoons in their hands. There was a lot of noise and many odors.

I returned home late that afternoon. I lay down and looked at the ceiling. I closed my eyes. I thought. I talked with myself about things that were supposed to be the most important in human life. I concluded once again, "All this makes no sense at all." None of it. Life. Can anyone add anything to it? A good few months ago I had chosen the day when I would commit suicide. I was glad I had chosen it with such precision: the year, the month, the day, and even the hour. It seemed to me that the decision untied my hands, so to speak, in relation to others and gave me freedom of movement. I said to myself, "I am not bound to anyone now. I do not care about anything under the sun."

I cannot, I want to say first of all, stand people. This lack of sympathy for others of his kind is most certainly the main feature of contemporary man. It is not so bad as long as men get along: at such times they can still smile. But try to enter a crowded bus. They will look at you with fury and disgust. Only idiots crack jokes and make faces. The rest of the people look with dull indifference at the dirty windows. When I am in a bad mood I look at people as if they were a heap of live manure. I do not exclude myself, of course. Why should I respect and love others when I myself am a mere nothing and look upon myself with hate. They are not worse than I, to be sure, but neither are they better.

These feelings have not, however, any bearing on my behavior. I cannot kick a small child even though I know there is nobody around. Filled with the worst words and the basest repulsion, I bend down to pick up the glove of this or that woman, literally reeking of perfume. There are, nevertheless, hidden possibilities in man compared with which Raskolnikov's sin is like the sin of a small boy who has broken a flowerpot.

In any case, the times when men were demons have passed. Today even the greatest criminals turn out to be mere rags who maintain that only circumstance has made them murderers. Rudolf Hess, the Commandant of Auschwitz, wrote in his diary: "Please do not, while using these notes, reveal to the public eye all that which connects me with my wife and my children, all my soft impulses and most hidden doubts. Let the public see in me only a bloodthirsty beast, a cruel sadist and murderer of millions. For otherwise the people at large will not be able to imagine the Commandant of Auschwitz. They will never understand that he also had a heart and was not all evil." I hold these words to be the most horrible charge against contemporary man. He also had a heart. But let us return to our petty, everyday and rather boring affairs.

I ask myself questions and give myself honest answers. Perhaps these deliberations of a student of the humanities will help various psychologists, sociologists, theologians and other scientists and scholars see more clearly the world we live in. I am one of you, I am a human being. To tell you the truth, I have met others who are worse than I. I am an average young man who was eighteen when the war broke out.

Thus I lay in my room and thought to myself. I thought that if a group of people, "old men, women and children," were placed in front of me at a distance, say, of one hundred yards, and a machine gun given to me with the order to shoot, I would shoot without asking any questions. It would be enough for me to wear a uniform and for the order to come from my superiors. I think that the Nazis were murderers, but we, their victims, with some resistance no doubt and not quite of our own free will, can change into murderers also.

I would fire a few rounds on that crowd of "old men, women and children" and that would be it. I think that, from such a distance, one would be able to kill a considerable number of people without a sick stomach and dizzy head . . . The airmen who destroyed whole cities had, I am quite sure, certain airs of elegance and dignity which distinguished them from other soldiers. The important thing is not to dirty your hands with the blood of those you kill or tangle your feet in the intestines of your victims. These are, after all, aesthetic, or perhaps also hygienic, considerations. Granted that not all of us are able to engage in hand-to-hand combat or to inflict torture on others; every man is capable, however, of causing death from a distance. Tearing a child to pieces with your own hands is, after all, something other than shooting from afar. Because, when you consider it more closely, even in peacetime wives cut their husbands to pieces and distribute their dismembered bodies in railroad stations and cinemas. So perhaps we should not exaggerate so much about the war. It may very well all be a question of quantity, don't you think?

All right, I have earned the right to go on about myself. There I lay on the bed and thought. I thought to myself that here they were, all these different pieces of furniture, books and pictures, but together they made no sense at all. Here I am, lying in bed, and this does not make any sense either. When I cease eating, washing, reading, talking and buying— what shall I do then? It is a pity that I cannot express it better. Let us hope that something will come of this story, after all.

Now, I am lying on my bed. And how am I lying? I am lying so intensely, I feel this lying so strongly that I practically have become one with the bed. I enjoy and delight in my position. I have turned the key in the lock and put on the lamp, covered with a hood made from an old newspaper. No one will come into my room, no one will throw me out of bed, and no one will tell me to go out into the darkness and the rain. No one will kick me and no one will slap my face. I can go on lying here for one, two, five hours if I want to. Later I will get up and eat. Hot, juicy sausages. They are now warming in the saucepan. No one will take my sausages, my tea and my bread away from me.

I have swallowed two sausages already, devoured them in an instant; the next pair I eat slowly, savoring the juices. I can eat at least a dozen of them by midnight. Tomorrow I can buy some more, as well as some rolls and a bottle of fruit wine. I can lock myself in, eat and lie in bed all day long; I can eat, lie on my bed and read an old newspaper in which one of my books is wrapped. It appears that the news of a year ago is just as interesting as the news of yesterday. Perhaps even more interesting if it comes to that. Events are illusory. Everything has stopped and I am pleased it has. The dead are buried. Those who are living no longer die. Perhaps they will never die. Below, in the restaurant, one can still talk with the cook

17

and the girls who clean the house. Talk and laugh. These women are gay and joyful, as if they were born yesterday or came from a different planet. It is enough to make a joke about something they have between their legs and they burst out laughing. Life conquers death. Love conquers death. Poor death—we turn away our eyes from her. People have had enough of her.

But I do not go below. I stay in my little hole. I lie on my bed and read the old newspaper. I close my eyes and wonder whether I have any desires. I have no wishes whatever. Or perhaps only one: let nobody enter here. I want to stay here just the way I am now. I do not want to go to America or to the moon. I do not want to go to an opera house, talk in any cafe, I do not want to be a movie actor or a king. I want nothing. I feel so good I do not even feel my own existence. I do not have to fight for my existence. I have a home, food, clothing, a bed, a stove and plenty of fuel to keep myself warm.

Early in the evening I went out and bought some sausages. Carrying them in a bag, I ran back home like a dog with meat between his teeth being chased by a butcher. I am still very happy every time I manage to get some food. I still fear that it will suddenly become scarce or that my house will fall down on me. I am terrified every time I return home: terrified that I will see its walls broken with charred windows, or a heap of broken stones and tangled wires and pipes. The discovery that my home is intact, even after a week's absence, or that I can open the door to my room, fills me with profound pleasure. The key. And on top of that, the house.

I open my wardrobe and once again check the contents of the paper box, covered with black English letters. For two days now I have been spreading out—on the bed and the table —the whole lot of small boxes, bags and cans. I even have chewing gum.

These nocturnal deliberations have no value whatever. Nothing ever comes of them. When day comes they die with the moon. I used to compose farewell letters, but I have gotten over this now. For, to be truthful, I have nothing at all to tell other people. Nothing wise or desperate. Now people should die silently. It is more decent this way. One should, as a matter of fact, open one's mouth only when it is absolutely necessary. Thus I will go away without sharing with anyone either my wisdom or my cry of despair. Although, to be frank, nothing disastrous has ever happened to me. I will go away, die that is, simply because I have come to the conclusion that I may or may not be here tomorrow. I might die, but then so might these five men and two women who are now making so much noise downstairs. All of us might die and never again appear in this house. Let them die or live; your, my or her life or death has no meaning for others . . . It is altogether impossible to compose a whole out of fragmentary deeds, words and ideas.

I have often asked myself: would I have any last wish before my death? Would I ask for anything before I die? My answer has always been the same: nothing, nothing at all. And yet I sometimes suspect that this is precisely the new meaning of our times: for those who come after us nothing will be clear any more. In the past, people wrote farewell letters, signed last wills, and even composed inscriptions for their tombstones. Our generation died modestly. This we have never forgotten.

Mistaken are those who say that now, after the war, many difficult moral issues have sprung into being. There is only life and it knows no morality. There are still some remnants, fragments and recollections of old morality, but one lives, so to speak, apart from them. People live and die. Everything has been explained ultimately. We understand everything.

We are also, all of us postwar people, suspect: heroes and traitors, conspirators and usurers, blackmailers and blackmailed, provocateurs, torturers and their victims. Even the dead are suspect. We all have been poisoned: the dead and the living. It is, of course, possible that my image of these things is false, I do not deny this. I say what I think. I want to write this deposition before I die. It might be of use to those who believe in men and have hope. Though I do not know anybody like that.

I should not talk about other people, however. It is of myself that I must speak. Speak for yourself. Let everyone speak only for himself. It may be that there are good and bad people—it is no longer important. Let them be. We go on. "We die insignificantly on the edge of the well of life and truth." I read this in a poem by some nineteenth century poet. Since then it has been explained that there is no "well of life and truth."

I do not think there was anyone in the corridor when I began to talk loudly to myself. And even if there had been anyone there—so what? I talked to myself as if to another man, an enemy and a scoundrel. I spoke with contempt and hate. My words were not fragments of one logical whole. "You dung heap," I said, "dung heap, dung heap. Swine. Damned creature. Horror. Oh, if only all of it could end. Damn you. There, you dirty swine. There, you coward," I shouted and slapped my face. Then I began to weep. I wept into my pillow and there was in this weeping some kind of solution and explanation. It is children who cry most often.

I washed my face in cold water. I wanted to run out and visit my friend. I will tell him all about it, I said to myself. I even began to put on my jacket, but then took it off and hung it on the nail. No one will help you. Don't you remember? He is the man who sought help from others, ran all over the place, drank vodka, painted his face with mustard. And now you want to run to him? Sit where you are. Weep and wait. He is a moralist. It was he who once briefly defined the meaning of life: eating, sleeping and copulating. I respect him. He is able, diligent, honest. He really has many virtues. And yet that was the way he described the meaning of life. I was shocked. Do I reproach him for what he said? No. He said it with conviction.

2.

The woman who lives next door to me will die soon. Let her die. Meanwhile, she is still strong enough and, lying in bed, swears at everybody in and out of her sight. She calls even me "a swine." She keeps on shouting behind the door, "swine, swine," and I know that she means me. I do not blame her at all and even smile in a friendly way as I pass along the dark corridor, listening to her squeaking voice. I do my best to be quiet. I walk on my toes, shut my door very carefully, do not play the radio, do not bring girls to my room and do not drink. I know that she keeps saying "cattle, cattle, cattle" again and again out of her anger with the world. Thus her life ends. She suffers. She apparently has nothing nice or pleasant to say to anyone. Bravo, my old woman, you are sincere. There she is, dying, but she does not lie. One must express one's feelings toward "mankind" briefly and to the point. "Mankind" does not take offense even at that. It is tolerant or, better still, indifferent. "The cattle" go on and are so busy that they pay no attention to your most vicious words. The accounts have been settled. Die. There never will be any shortage of men.

Is this how it is then? You probably know the saying: "If only I could be born again! My life would be altogether different." It is one of the most ridiculous platitudes in the world. I am not a bad man. I know that it has no meaning whether I am good or bad, but still I repeat: I am not a bad man. Wouldn't it be better for me to live and work believing in mankind's "sunny future" rather than thinking about having to drown or hang myself? Perhaps in a lavatory?

The night is getting deeper. In the sky there are clouds and black, thin images of poplar trees. I can hear the distant sound of roaring. The windows are shut and people go to sleep. I myself do not want to sleep, I am afraid to. Now one should live continuously, sit up with one's eyes open and think. How long can one go to sleep and wake up without hope? I am still alive and intend to live for some time, but I no longer am here. It is a horrible feeling. I would rather have people spit at me, walk over me and throw dirty words at me: I would feel alive. My existence must be confirmed constantly by others.

Below, the restaurant is quiet. The lights have been shut off and the girls have gone to sleep. It is raining. The rain falls hard on the cement tiles of the courtyard.

Oh, to leave my clothing, books, identifications. To leave name, acquaintances, "environment." To leave the entire past behind. There is only the present and the future, which is being born every minute and which I do not know. I must go through my future myself. Oh, to break the chains and escape. I do not want to attend lectures tomorrow. There is no university and there is no architecture of the Italian Renaissance. There is no city of Paris. When I was alive I wanted to see the city of Paris. A distant city. I regarded those who had been there as people from a different planet. I would ask them to send me letters describing the air, street corners, flowers and rubbish, pictures and hats. I no longer care about such things. It is not true that you have just returned from Paris. Please do not tell me anything about that city. I know it does not really exist. You are all part of the plot: you talk about the theatres, picture exhibitions, the Seine and red wine, but I know that Paris has never existed. If it had, my street would not be so grey and I would be happier. My father and my grandfather never saw the city of Paris either. Here we have a courtyard surrounded by a wall made of red bricks; the bricks have been laid so tight that you cannot see anything through them. I, myself, have always stood with my face close to the wall.

My neighbor has been running since early dawn. His trembling face is changing into a dog's muzzle. He runs up and down the corridor with his metal can, which previously contained lemon juice; in it, he carries water to the toilet. The pipes have broken down again, and again the inhabitants of this huge house have to smell their own odors. This in itself is enough to wipe the smiles off their faces and they no longer say good day to each other. My neighbor's daughter, sad, flat-chested and dressed in a black, shiny apron, stands guard at the toilet door, making sure that nobody forgets to flush his or her excrement. Violent quarrels flare up. Beautiful volumes, published by Insel-Verlag zu Leipzig, Rilke, Plato, Schopen-hauer, stand on that gentleman's bookshelves: he has been feeding his whole, anemic life on the poetry of Claudel, Mal-larme, Nerval . . . and now, angry as a village dog, he runs up and down the stinking corridor, gnashing his teeth. He is ready to bite. I lie in my bed and listen to this cultured fam-ily's canine exercise. A moment ago the toilet was used by an old woman who did not flush her excrement. Though she will die soon, she now trembles with fear in her bed.

The subtle gentleman roars, "Pigs, pigs," and I know that he addresses not only me and my neighbors, but the whole of mankind.

"Poor man," I think of him with pity and a dose of spite, "he has wasted the best years of his life on intellectual talk and now must make up for it. It is a pity he does not have any teeth, because then he would be able to bite the door-knob or the wall."

Again the corridor is quiet. Again the house is quiet. It has stopped raining and I can see the dark poplar trees against the dirty, silver-turning sky.

3.

Dead we live. Shrewd, spiteful, treacherous, knowing what's what, decomposing—we live. We, the dead. We know each other well and we know the secret well. They say that rebellious poets and artists at the end of the last century used to escape to Africa . . . We also can rebel. Do you see those quiet people with the stupid expressions on their faces—they also are rebels, but no one knows about it. Already quiet and tamed, they wait in the streets for the policeman's signal, the green light. Only sometimes they vomit, drunk, and show their fists to their enemies, art, God. In most cases, another man's wife, a brief and vulgar conquest and fall is enough to bring them back to reality. Others used to escape to Africa or to the South Sea islands. Where shall we escape to? To the Equator perhaps? No, we escape to our bathrooms. It turns out, however, that bathrooms are not as peaceful and quiet as they used to be. We look at each other suspiciously: who will pay for repairs? We look at each other angrily. You can't always tell who is guilty of leaving his excrement. Should one escape into oneself then? Surely, it is better to escape to a waiting room at the railroad station of Gorzkowice. We know our inner selves too well, the inner faces of contemporary men. Who can bear being alone with his inner self for one lonely evening, one sleepless night? My life has been deprived of sense. When the time of test came I fought with a rifle in my hand and "shed blood"; thus I have done my duty to myself, to my people and my country. But I have failed to save the sense of my life.

Everything is finished once and for all, whatever I may do. I am dead. Who again dares to speak about music and poetry, to whisper about beauty? Who again speaks about man? Who dares to speak about man? What buffoonery, what comedy! You, the dead! I am with you. How fine I feel.

The poor old woman had had her eye on my room. She knew that I intended to move out of this huge house. She planned to fix her kitchen in my room. She died on the day I was packing my suitcases. It seems that she spent two days and two nights dying. Though, I must admit, I know nothing for certain about that. It happened quietly, behind closed doors.

Our corridor was narrow and crowded with old furniture. I heard sounds, as if someone were moving wooden boxes from one place to another. I opened the door but had to shut it immediately. The door came up against the coffin in which the old woman was being carried away. The coffin had stuck and they could not get it out. They bumped against the walls, furniture and doors. I saw the yellow-lacquered coffin and heard the men's tired breathing. Finally, after some time, they managed to squeeze the coffin through and then I heard their footsteps on the stairs. I sat on my bed—on its mattress as hard as planks. I fell asleep and lived here for some time. Perhaps several years. My two suitcases, packed and closed, stood against the wall.

When I first came I hoped that here, in this new house and among strangers, I would find a man who would help me come back to life. Instead they all wept, vomited and confided in their women. I soon began to feel disgust. Later, all through these years, we passed each other like strangers.

These were long periods when everything seemed unreal. People were made—as far as I was concerned—only of skin and meat and I suspected there was nothing inside them. I was interested in finding the soul. It was all rather macabre. In the heads of these people were mouths, which almost never shut, and in these mouths large numbers of bad teeth. All of these people spoke a lot. These were the first postwar years. They talked so much that, finally, everything they said became very confusing. For many years, every discussion left people more and more ignorant of what it was all about. Among them were Catholics, Communists and those who, before your very eyes, changed from Catholics into Communists. There were among them ordinary worms, sponges, and the devil knows what, old people, young people, idiots, moralists, and many others. It is quite clear that my experiences have not been limited exclusively to the inhabitants of the house I lived in. I mentioned them only by the way, because, in the final score, they interested me no more than any other people in the world. If I mention them it is because I have lived next door to them for a longer time. I saw too clearly, I am sure of that. In the faces of the people I met at that time I was interested only in the eyes. These eyes often had a wild, hard, contemptuous and cruel look about them. On both sides of their heads all the people I met had ears. These ears looked especially comical on men wearing hats. They grew out, these naked, white and red ears, each on its own side of the head. I must admit that I was quite amused, sometimes at least, by their noses. Growing out from somewhere between their eyes, these noses seemed to have a shape which obviously must have been the result of Nature's humor or negligence. The noses came out of the faces aggressively. In addition, the people I met each had a pair of legs and a pair of arms. They used their legs quite naturally and modestly, but their arms and hands seemed to give them a lot of trouble. Even the people I took for being quite intelligent and educated did not know what to do with their arms and hands. They either put them in their pockets or carried them around, locked, on their behinds. Sometimes they put them on their hips, but this made even less sense. Some people seemed to find a way out of this embarrassing situation by using their hands for holding newspapers, gloves or walking sticks. Another way was to walk arm in arm. As soon as the hands were empty, however, the trouble and the confusing search began.

Their heads were covered with hair. I also saw people who cultivated—just above their upper lip—thin, sharp moustaches. I try very hard to describe and to explain these different stages of my "clear seeing," but I know that I am only confusing everything. Man will die and never succeed in describing the important things. One dies mute. Man talks for fifty years and all his words, from the first to the last, turn finally into a horrible bellowing. People speak too much and all at once. Everyone waits for his chance to have his say in full. I passed these people as one passes a closed newspaper stand.

Because one of my acquaintances had admission cards to the Philharmonic, I sometimes went to listen to concerts. If I remember correctly I listened one evening to Beethoven's Ninth Symphony. On the stage, I saw the various members of the orchestra, dressed in black suits. They sat before their stands and held various instruments. Later they played. I sat and looked at the choir. Old, poor angels in white skirts . . . The choir sang a *pathetique* and it seemed as if all these poorly paid performers wanted to enter heaven. In the last row of musicians sat a neatly barbered man with a black moustache. With an incorruptible dignity, he beat on his drum. He resembled Hitler. I was rather bored and even suffered a little. The Symphony was definitely too long. Anyway, the hall was very warm and not ventilated. I felt that I was listening to tremendous music, great to be sure, but devoid of sense and meaning, at least for me. For we never will enter heaven despite the trying efforts of the martyrs of art. Music is like a cathedral which, standing high on a hill, dominating a city, is yet of much less importance than, say, a municipal slaughterhouse, stadium, cinema or water reservoir. I am, of course, quite aware that this comparison between the cathedral and the slaughterhouse is artificial, demagogic and obviously stupid.

Although at that time I was twenty-five years old I wanted to learn and understand the purpose for which we lived. With the stubbornness of a child, I waited for a revelation. I had asked other people about it in the past, but had given this up because soon it seemed strange and comical to me.

There were, I assure you, whole periods of complete death in my life. I was not. At such times I would begin to move violently from one place to another, and even to act. I wanted to know for certain that I existed. I tried to make new acquaintances—on trains and in the streets. I even waited to meet and to speak to other men, complete strangers, on the stairs. It seemed to me that I had to deliver speeches, take part in discussions, and put my hand on a certain woman's knee.

At such times I would pack my suitcases and go to the railroad station, walk around there for hours and return home, tired. I would even visit public lavatories so that I could listen there to the voices of life.

Supplication

I want to be alone. When I hear a knock on the door I hold my breath and do not move. Someone is waiting there, I know. Someone wants me to open the door. I make him think I have left.

I have become so disgusted with people that I choose to be alone. But I also have learned to hate myself. Constantly, I repeat to myself, "Why have you not died, why have you not died?" The moments when I feel I do not exist are terrifying. Although I sit in my chair, lie down, read or listen to lectures, I am not really in any of these places. Nature has so disgusted me that I have not been in the forest or in the field for years. I have not seen flowers, bees, butterflies, and instead stare intensely at my old lamp, covered with soot, and at the pile of old, yellow newspapers.

Alone. I thought that man could be alone. Now, however, I run out of the house and am on the brink of madness. Now I run out to be near people. How good it feels to be pushed, how good it feels to be among the wicked, impatient bodies. At last, I am with you. I am with you forever. Do not leave me alone. I was conceited and stupid. I am waiting now. I yearn for a living man. I wait for his coming. Every sound in the courtyard and every clatter of footsteps on the staircase makes my heart beat faster. I hold my breath.

Let him be that little, dirty man whose mouth smells. I would not greet the sight of new lands, or stars, or mountain tops, with such cries of joy as I would give him. It is for him I wait on this autumn day, so many years after the war.

I do not need God, gold, fame. The man who consents to come into my room does not have to be Einstein, Napoleon, Socrates . . . If only he will keep his promise, that old friend of mine: old, bitter, angry, smelling of rags and beer. We will sit at the table, he and I, and smoke cheap cigarettes and repeat to each other poor truths, gossip and regrets. He will tell me how brave, helpful, noble and talented he is, how different he is from other people. He will never even imagine how grateful I am to him for coming. He will never know that I regard him as a golden god, my creator, benefactor and savior. I will look at him with hidden joy and be grateful to him for sitting here with me, for being.

But he does not come.

He does not know that he is as necessary as air, water, food and light. He surely would come if he knew.

Around eleven at night it gets cold and empty. I sit in the electric light and there is darkness outside. I lock my door and slowly walk down the stairs. I stop. I listen.

NOVEMBER 1955—DECEMBER 1956.

Translated by Paul Mayewski

The Defense of Granada

1.

Olek Yust was standing at the Foksal Street trolley stop, hands in his pockets, staring at the sun. His clothes showed that he had attended the recent Youth Festival: he was wearing an orange shirt with green stripes, which he had got from a Norwegian, and a pair of shabby corduroy trousers. "What's new?" I asked. "Thomas Mann died," he said. "That was more than a month ago," I said. "Don't you think I read the papers?"

Scooping a handful of pistachio nuts out of a pocket, he repeated:

"Thomas Mann died. It's all our fault, of course. Everybody has a little beard and cries, 'Look what you've done! The peasants don't trust you, you didn't publish The Complete Works of Conan Doyle, and it's your fault that Thomas Mann died.' You say you read the papers. Well, then you know who gave the lecture at the memorial meeting at the Institute—our old friend, Doctor Faul."

Awkwardly, he walked away, the passers-by turning curi-

ously to look at his tall frame, his striped shirt, and his face of
a mournful spaniel.

"Yust!" I called after him, "Yust, wait!"

*

In these pages there will be mention of Doctor Faul, as he
came to be called. His real name had a different sound. But
he was regarded as a clever man; today, some people say that
he was too clever, even a cheat. I suppose that was the origin
of the nickname, launched, no doubt by a wiseacre, a few
months ago. Before that he was merely referred to as "the
Doctor," although he did not like to use the title himself.

His appearance made you wonder. No particular features
—but that was what struck you. It would be hard to say what
he looked like. Someone, meeting him for the first time, once
said: "Mr. Anonymous in person!" He was medium size, gray
in color, and, as though having no eyes of his own, looked at
you through glasses that revealed a reduced reflection of
yourself rather than anything behind them. He dressed carefully, and the indefinite shades of Polish-made cloth blended
with his hair. I repeat: he was striking in his very lack of anything striking. If his face had belonged to another man, I
should not have been able to recall it. But because it was his,
we remember it.

The people at the Institute spoke of him with caution.
He did not bully his subordinates. Julka Glinska, who had
been in his office two or three years, said: "Once a week he
inquired about my little boy, and asked me if the streetcar
had been crowded." She lost her job—a day or so after her
husband was arrested—on grounds of "staff reorganization."
It was I who got her the job of secretary at the Granada.

*

In 1945 ten generations of young people had emerged
from the war—ten generations rather different from our own.
During the war they had been educated at breakneck speed—
it was like a very special Five-Year Plan. For five years, every
day of their lives had been crowded with experiences, each of

which, taken separately, could have filled a whole lifetime. The subjects they had been taught were Death, Love and Hunger; their classrooms had been streets and courtyards. Everything had gone into those five years, and then everything was lost. Never before had the world seen such veterans. They flocked back disorganized, and set about reconstructing daily life out of nothing. They returned still dazzled by the brilliance of their fiery adventures, but already bitter at the thought of their futility. Olek Yust told me: "We were off on a drunken spree. It was like a night of oblivion. And then we had to pay for it."

They had learned a lot about mankind—for instance, that people could be processed into soap. They had learned more or less the same about their nation. They belonged to a nation that might have perished. What was left was a strong appetite for life, and because they had nothing else, because they were disillusioned, they felt they had little to say. "After five years of war, we don't know how to speak. We can only cry, 'Never again!' Please, teach us how to speak, we want to use human language, to be able to distinguish good from evil, yes from no, to say 'this is the sky and this is the earth,' or even just to say simple things, like 'Ala goes to the woods.' Please, create an alphabet for us, write it out in large, distinct letters, teach us, human beings, how to speak."

The men who asked this of the new era were answered. The era was not deaf to their request: they were presented with the alphabet of revolution.

Revolution—as we all know now—can take many forms, but there is one thing revolution must guard against—pettiness. Each of its days must amaze us, carry us forward. Not for nothing has it been compared to a train, "the speeding train of history." The laggards must not be given a moment's respite. If backward elements are allowed to take the floor, if their voice can be heard, something is wrong with the wheels of the train. The history of the Granada Theater is a case in point.

The Granada Theater was founded by three men. In the

ruins of a building in Polna Street part of a former movie house had survived. There were weeds in the orchestra pit, and on the balcony a wild pear tree offered shade from the sun. Those young men wanted their own theater. At first they devoted evenings to the memory of the Uprising, reciting *Polish Flowers* to its veterans, and girls wept. But they wanted a theater. Some of them had brief experience at a dramatics school, and could recite Norwid from memory; but apart from that they knew very little—how to pick fights over Poland, and throw bottles at tanks. They made benches out of old boards and patched up the roof, and girls painted the walls.

They got some help, a little money, and a permit from the Ministry. Thus the Granada company was gradually assembled. At once it was referred to as "a young poetic stage." In the long, narrow auditorium there were readings of Mayakovsky, Svetlov, and younger poets. Boys with disheveled hair would sing out, "May I have the floor?" The discussions continued till late at night. In Warsaw people began to say that predatory chicks had built themselves a nest in Polna Street.

Suddenly poems were not enough. They had become Communists, no one knew just when, and a revolutionary theater was in the air. Jokes about them circulated in cafés. Doubts were expressed that they ever brushed their teeth; and one of them was quoted as having said, "Oh, Shakespeare!" Their critics underestimated the solidarity of these young people who trusted only each other and were suspicious of those whose war experiences had been different from their own. Everywhere they scented tricks—they had been taken for a ride once. They could not be bribed with either money or sentiment, having paid the highest price for survival itself. Even now they were not thanked too cordially for their past exploits: they had still to account for their wounds. Although their attitude to the new era was one of harsh resignation, it whetted their curiosity. They greeted the revolution with respectful attention: the armored car with the flying red flag looked interesting. The transports they had traveled in had

33

been smashed; this was shiny, efficient-looking, new. They longed for a serious fight, and they needed authoritative leadership. Romantic, embittered adventurers, they were ready to turn in their tin and cardboard equipment for the real thing, a ride on the train to new adventure.

2.

"We're going to kick the petty bourgeoisie in the groin, they've had it coming to them for a long time. You think we'll soften up, but you're mistaken. There is no such thing as a gentle revolution. Precisely because ours was bloodless, it must speak to them with a gun pointing at their heads. Do you know the play? Come to the reading, Polna Street. I see you're smiling. Nobody will be smiling on opening night, will they, Yust?"

The speaker was Piotr Slawski, one of the "three." This was the summer of 1949, and in the fall the Granada Theater was to stage Mayakovsky's play, *The Bath*. I had not smiled, but Slawski had throughout. This was the sort of thing they did then, provoking discussion all over the city, especially seeking out the undecided. Contemptuous, they did not withhold all hope of heaven: you don't like it, you don't trust us, then at least come to Polna Street, to the Granada, we'll talk, and you'll see for yourself whether we are young barbarians.

The rehearsals were at night. Slawski, a little man, locked the doors of the auditorium, and they drank buckets of black coffee. He had fought in the Old City during the Uprising, had come to Polna Street in the uniform of a militia lieutenant, and was perhaps the only one among them all who did not feel disappointed in some way. He gave them their style—jeering, truthful, merciless towards weakness. The nightly rehearsals were like courtroom proceedings; he would accuse them of reading badly, because they did not believe what they were saying. Gradually they became like him; in time the differences between them were wiped out, they even looked alike:

thin, restless, without neckties, with big clumsy hands that they liked to hide in their pockets. Andrzej T——, when caught with a girl backstage, was expelled from the company. Firmly, they consolidated their ideological unity. Jacek Woynar, one of the "three", was made to separate from his wife who worked at the Swedish Embassy. The Party meetings would last till dawn; they did not indulge in horseplay. In September, administration of the Granada was taken over by the Institute, and Swatkowski and Miernik came to one of the rehearsals.

The two were Doctor Faul's closest collaborators in the I.O.K., the Institute for Cultural Organizations, which for several months had been housed in a newly-rebuilt palace. Its personnel comprised several hundred persons, all of whom carried out the Plan in silence. Thick carpets muffled the footsteps of the secretaries; the new copper roof, according to calculations by specialists, would soon acquire its patina. A patina—that was what the palaces of our new institutions were still lacking. Swatkowski and Miernik appeared in the company of Rena Szulc, drama critic of *The Week*. They were smaller than she—you know Rena Szulc, the powerful brunette with big breasts. They listened to the play and inspected the theater. Rena had tears in her eyes. They nodded, and observed, "Very interesting." The company appreciated their cautious reticence. They impressed everyone as serious. Next day the rumor got around that rehearsals of *The Bath* had been stopped.

Then Piotr saw Julka Glinska for the first time. He put his hand on her desk: "Tell them, Comrade, that the Granada delegation has arrived." "I announced them, they didn't have to wait long," she recalled later.

An hour later they left the Doctor's office, pale, silent, and convinced. In saying "convinced," I have in mind that feeling of a specifically inner weakening that we all experience when confronted with a "higher reason." In all of nature there is no more helpless creature than a man afflicted with the curse of honesty. It is easy to reach him, easy to undermine his certainty—because, not knowing the ultimate consequences of his actions, he is always ready to doubt them. He is perpetually asking himself questions, and not finding answers to all of them; he is always anxious to know whether he has acted well, and whether his goals are socially useful. Often the question, "What for?" or "Whom does it favor?" or "What does it accomplish?" suffices to introduce a sneaking, cold apprehension into his innermost being, an apprehension that neither plants nor animals know: "I was mistaken, my ideas are good for nothing and no one."

I was not present at that discussion, but I have attended a hundred similar ones, and the method is familiar to me. Doctor Faul would have asked them a few questions, and then answered them himself. The gray figure in glasses, with the calm voice of a mathematics teacher, would not arouse suspicion. Were they aware of the ultimate consequences of their actions? Every idea expressed is an action, every single one of our actions has a thousand consequences, and ultimately affects production. Were they aware of their political responsibility for the word? Between the word and its consumers, processes of a new type are today taking place, processes that must be taken into account. One of the features of political irresponsibility is that it succumbs to the magic of concepts. Mayakovsky was a giant of the revolution, it is true. But this giant arose under certain specific circumstances, which are historically unrepeatable. Art has no super-temporal function; the crushing foot of this giant might destroy you. Yes, we are concerned with the masses, how very true. But are you absolutely certain of what best serves the interests of the masses at the present stage of the historical process? We have complete certainty. The working class does not always realize its own interests with sufficient clarity—we, however, see them clearly at every given moment. Today the masses must be presented with images of production, the people must be made to love production, the work of its own hands. Whatever does not contribute to this end is unusable. The unusable is our enemy. Your arguments were answered long ago, your ideas are filed away in one of my drawers, you only have the illusion that you are discovering the world. You say, *"The Bath,"* "Maya-kovsky," "the anger of a great tree-chopper against the small chips of the revolution"—it all sounds very pretty. But I put to you the question: What for? Whom does this serve today? Have you forgotten that the enemy never sleeps? Are we not working for the enemy? Think it over, comrades.

Think it over: try to separate what is true from what may be only a conjurer's trick, an ideological sleight-of-hand. The founders of the Granada Theater were short of arguments. There they sat, crushed by the weight of all these unfamiliar ideas, thinking that this little man whose eyes were perpetually hidden behind thick glasses was probably the greatest expression of the epoch. Renowned magicians and other masters of illusion make use of precision instruments; they too are quite capable of creating masterpieces of efficiency. This only requires modern technology, and the knowledge of the laws of physics and psychology. Their magic passes cannot be perceived by the naked eye, because they practice in front of mirrors so long that in the end they can't even see through themselves. Was Doctor Faul one of these? Had he, constantly verifying his method before the mirror of objective laws, ceased in the end to perceive the slight motion of his own hand by which appearance was transformed into fact—had he fallen for it? Woe unto them of little faith, for more than one thing may be pulled out of their sleeves!

After leaving the office, Slawski, Yust and Woynar did not go right back to the Granada. The rest of the company was waiting in Polna Street, and not one of them was willing to believe that the suspension of rehearsals could be anything but a malicious rumor. For an hour the "three" sat on a bench in Lazienki Park; it began to rain; at moments they felt as though they had committed treason. They tried to remember all of the Doctor's arguments, and were tormented by the fear that they had not exhausted their own. He had drawn before their eyes an irrefutably logical figure, a perfectly coherent design in which every part confirmed the whole, just as the whole confirmed every part. Now they had become one of those parts, he had locked them up inside this perfect whole, and they dared not suspect a trick.

He had asked them for sacrifices, however, and for these they were strong enough. Still, what he demanded was the greatest sacrifice of all: they had to destroy their very dreams, together, and with their own hands; they had to dismantle one edifice, and in its place erect another; and they themselves, with their own hands, had to bolt all the exits. They were exhausted in advance. In their ears there still rasped the dry voice pronouncing all those words that mankind uses to define the problems of its existence—the nation, work, history. . . . There were three of them. Each had committed at least one mistake in his life. None wanted to be cut off from the truth of his era. They loved the dark and complicated twentieth century. That is why they now sat on a bench in Lazienki Park, wondering anxiously whether the sacrifice being asked of them was truly in the spirit of the century.

A few days later two new members were added to the administration of the Granada Theater—Swatkowski and Miernik.

3.

To the memory of Anton Chekhov

The two were not at all alike, yet outwardly they appeared the same. They were rarely seen separately, even though they were not supposed to be seen together; at such times they formed two parts of one somewhat embarrassed whole. They made few unnecessary movements, and their taciturn reserve gave them the festive dignity of tailors, but somewhere far below the surface of their pale glances was concealed an anxious knowledge of experiences in which they had both probably been involved.

In the spring they had accompanied an official delegation to the German People's Republic. In Berlin, lured by a desire to bite into the rotten apple of capitalism, Miernik went on his own to the Western sector. He walked along the Kurfürstendamm, somewhat shocked by his own boldness, for at every step he saw the very phenomena that he had condemned in articles and speeches. A momentary shiver ran down his spine: what would Swatkowski say? After all, they knew each other very well. This thought somehow depressed him; he began to look about for the shortest way back, when by chance his eyes rested on a large window display in a corner store, and there Miernik saw a hat.

There were many other things in the shop window, but Miernik was held by that hat, which was set off to advantage on an artfully-folded piece of white silk. He walked over to it, and began to examine it, rather against his will. The hat was exceptionally lovely, Miernik had to admit no other word would do. Dark green, with an unusually smooth finish, a gently curved brim, and a narrow band; it was a felt hat. He recalled the hat his father used to wear on Sundays; he remembered it clearly from childhood, but this one was certainly superior— Miernik could not have said in just what way. He could not buy his father's hat, but he could buy this one—Eastern marks were accepted here. Despite himself, he had to smile, thinking of the correct path he had followed all his life, and he even felt a little proud of himself. He wanted to go away, it was really embarrassing standing like that in front of the window, but the hat held him. Even though Miernik recalled the number of unemployed in West Berlin, he could not take his eyes off it. Could he really buy it? He tried to imagine Swatkowski's face, were he to see him wearing it. Swatkowski would say nothing, perhaps would even pretend not to notice. That was what Miernik feared most—the hat's unfathomable consequences, the comments it would arouse, the moment when it would cease to be a mere head covering, and become an object calling for explanation. And rightly so: was it not a product of exploitation, intended for exploiters? Why, it was a standing argument of reactionary propaganda against Socialist production, even, to some extent, a symbol of capitalist encirclement. A fine thing, if he, Miernik, went back to the Institute with the very symbol of capitalist encirclement on his head! He moved away from the glass, but it drew him back again. The hat was beautiful, so different from Polish-made hats! "There you lie," Miernik thought, "and I stand looking at you. Separately we are merely a man and a hat. But if we joined forces, I would be a man in a hat, and you would be a datum in my personal history. Better lie peacefully there."

Suddenly he was seized with a violent longing for that piece of green felt. He would have it, have it as his property, have it for himself! True, he had an official car and was proud of it (though he had to share it with Swatkowski), and he also had a well-furnished office (though Swatkowski worked at an adjoining desk), movie tickets and invitations to the theater, and coupons for special stores (Swatkowski had them too)—but one decision could deprive him of all that. What would he be then? What would he have left? His thoughts? Miernik had long since renounced thoughts that he could not share with Swatkowski; he no longer had them even before falling asleep. Then what else, my God? Bonuses? Swatkowski got those, too.

Miernik was sure that he deserved more. After all, he belonged to the group of men of superior talents, and hence to the category of leaders, which should somehow be distinguishable to the eyes of society. If he had that green hat, it would indicate a special caprice testifying to the high degree of confidence, and even to a certain absentmindedness, in the man who besides his competence possesses a hat such as no one else wears. "Why don't I go in and try it on? After all,

I could keep it in the closet, and wear it only at home." The madness of this idea frightened him, and he resolved to leave the spot. And just then, by the trembling of his legs, he knew that he would do the exact opposite. Pale, dazed, he suddenly found himself inside the shop.

The hat fitted him perfectly, and Miernik stood in front of the mirror, disbelieving his own reflection. He felt positively dashing, and the salesgirl looked at him with admiration. He paid, said, "No, thank you," when she offered to wrap his purchase. He was reeling slightly when he walked out, holding the green hat delicately by two fingers; he feared to put a thing so shamelessly beautiful on his head. He had not walked twenty steps when he saw Swatkowski.

Miernik froze, but it was too late. Swatkowski must have come to catch him on the Kurfürstendamm, having scented something wrong. They greeted each other rather coolly.

"Ah," said Swatkowski, "hello."

Miernik's hands were sweating; in the left one, behind his back, he clutched the hat. Swatkowski pretended that he was not in the least surprised: this justified his worst fears. "What am I to do?" Miernik thought in a panic. "What am I to say? Can I conceal the hat to the last? Perhaps drop it? No, someone might pick it up." Swatkowski, too, was silent.

"What a lot of beggars," Miernik observed.

"Yes," Swatkowski said. "And a minimum of reconstruction. I took a walk over here because I have to give a lecture on capitalist economy at the Institute."

"A lecture!" Miernik groaned mentally. "You've been trailing me, you ox." He pressed the hat into the small of his back, and said: "That's interesting. *The Week* has asked me for an article on the same subject. That's why I dropped over here for a moment. Oh my, wasn't that a drop of water? God help me! But maybe the shower will miss us."

He was dimly aware that Swatkowski was watching him without, however, asking any questions. Miernik wished he could light a cigarette, but knew this was impossible—how could he light a cigarette with one hand? The hat was burning a hole in his back. He looked at Swatkowski's balding head with hatred—lucky man, he has nothing to cover it with, but then he has nothing to hide either. And he noticed that Swatkowski was looking at his own head, also balding. "It's raining," he realized with horror. "What will happen now?" Raindrops began to bounce on the sidewalk. The two men stood there face to face, shifting their weight from foot to foot. Swatkowski was waiting for something. Miernik suddenly realized what it was: "The rascal, he must have seen me walking out of the shop!" he lamented silently.

Then it really began to pour. Streams of water were slapping the marquee of the bar at the corner. There was nothing he could do, and anyway all was lost—he had to put his hat on. . . . Almost simultaneously they performed identical embarrassing motions with their left hands, revealing two identical dark green felt hats with narrow bands, each of which had been concealed behind their backs. On the deserted corner, with the rain coming down noisily, they stared at each other, utterly astonished.

4.

The scene is the Malgorzata mine in the Western Territories. Two brothers, named Chmar, work there. The elder Chmar is a foreman famous for his efficiency, the younger does not fulfill his quotas. The elder brother has a wife and two children, his wife being a devoted member of the Women's League. The younger brother drinks heavily in the company of one Mroczko, seduces girls, and tramples upon the pure love of Hanka, an "activist" of the Union of Polish Youth. The Chmars' bedridden mother, widow of a miner who had taken part in the Silesian insurrection, disowns her younger son for failing to fulfill his quotas. Through the work of the saboteur Mroczko, a disaster occurs in the mine. The older son, the foreman, is buried under the debris, and the younger son takes part in the rescue action. At the risk of his life the bad brother saves the good one. On hearing this, their mother, who has been gravely ill, recovers. The saboteur Mroczko, caught in a restaurant with a man in dark glasses, is arrested. The mother forgives her younger son, who has been poisoned by gas during the rescue operations (there is hope that he will recover), and the "activist" Hanka confesses that she had never stopped loving him. In the presence of Party officials and the elite of the miners, the Chmar brothers organize a shock brigade. Curtain.

Such was the plot of *Shock Brigade*, the new play that the Granada company was to produce. It had been recommended by the Institute. The script had been delivered by Rena Szulc.

"The Doctor has read it," she informed the company confidentially, "and had no reservations." Rena Szulc came to the Granada every day. She advised them to do the play, with all her great heart she advised them: "You'll strengthen your position, for the main problem today is coal. Coal is everything today." This Rena Szulc was not the worst kind. Slawski said to Yust: "Take her away from here. For heaven's sake, make her stop coming."

They refused to produce *Shock Brigade*. "It is too stupid," they said. "It was written by some bright boy who wants to cash in on the coal situation. We know how these things work."

They were a little unfair to the author. True, he wanted to cash in on the situation, but he took his work seriously. For some time he had been one of the parties to an unwritten collective contract. An important point in that secret contract proclaimed the childlike naiveté of the masses. The people was a child, one must speak to it in the language of children. The concept of the "new consumer," an essentially irrational creature, had been constructed. We have hundreds of thousands of youngsters who must be taught that fire burns, for otherwise they might set fire to the house. The man in the dark glasses is a wicked man, but the grandfather, the former rebel, was a very good man, and well-behaved children study their lessons. . . . O holy social pedagogy! So this is how you treat the people? The people which, according to your own teachings, is the eternal source of wisdom and the creator of experience? The people which possesses a knowledge of life as bitter as wormwood, and which has been spared nothing of life's shameful secrets? Divested of illusions and deprived of dreams, it has trained itself in irony, mistrusts ready-made truths intended for simpletons, and thirsts for knowledge. Let us not say in its name: This is what serves the objective interests of the masses, this is a popular hero, this is the people's optimism. Must the people be persuaded to love its own heroes and to desire its own victory? But today, when it has learned the rights to which it is entitled, when we ourselves inform it about the newly-exposed mysteries of matter, about the energy concealed in the smallest particles of being as well as in the immense nebulae of the universe, about artificial brains and the complications of economic life—today the common man wants to know. This is one of the rights he won for himself, a right he does not renounce, even temporarily.

The copy of Shock Brigade passed unhappily from hand to hand. They shrugged their shoulders: "It's unactable. The author should take up another profession." The author was referred to as Comrade Optimistenko, and his characters were ridiculed with eloquent quotations from The Bath. He was called a hairdresser giving reality a permanent wave, and his play a mixture of vaseline and hair oil. Is it our purpose to build socialism? In that case, let us speak the language of the revolution. The reaction, we are told, can destroy our people, yet at this point are we supposed to open a nursery school? Wouldn't you die of shame if those who were killed by Fascist bullets were resurrected to attend the performance of this play? Let us speak in full voice, let us teach hatred. We don't have to worry about love—love is implied in our Idea. "It will be produced in Bucharest," Swatkowski and Miernik said. "Oh, yes, in Bucharest. There was something about that in the newspapers."

Another conference in the Doctor's office. "The play *does* simplify things," he said. "That is true. We aren't giving you a golden apple, we are giving you a problem to solve. The hard raw material will soften in your hands, you'll break a new path. Others will follow you. Masterpieces are not created in times of social upheaval; it is a historical fact that art, after periods of flowering, often relapses into primitivism. The peasant is migrating to the city. It is the greatest migration in history: the people are moving on into the future. We must create a new catechism, formulate a new canon of social duties. Comrades Swatkowski and Miernik will acquaint you with the statistical figures, you should be familiar with these things. Mobilize the company. We'll break down the resistance of the intellectuals, and we'll help you, comrades."

The Doctor showed them the futility of their resistance. Only in the name of superior forces can a man speak with such calm. The fate and conscience of the individual mean little against such forces. He demonstrated the insignificance of individual conflicts; all other concerns, he said, must yield to the job of building socialism, a job that requires the efforts of millions. Man? Let us rather think of mankind. Man does not really exist, man is only a concept to be translated into reality, a mere working hypothesis. The spokesman for supra-individual rights thus demanded in their name that actual mankind be forgotten during the period dedicated to the construction of the new man.

Shock Brigade went into rehearsal late in November. Piotr Slawski read the script to the company. He sat alone at a table on the empty stage lit by a solitary bulb. After he was through, his glance slid over his listeners. They knew his sallow face with the gloomy flicker in the slanting eyes.

"This is required of us," he said. "We'll do everything we can. Anyone who doesn't feel strong enough, can get up and walk out now." No one moved. The parts were handed out.

5.

As soon as the play was cast, there began days of strenuous rehearsal. This was 1950. We shall remember those years for a long time to come. The final judgment on them has not yet been passed, and possibly it was one of those periods in which opposing forces clash openly, and which will always be argued about. In such epochs good and evil give battle to man in new ways, in unexpected places. Never having been attacked from this side before, man must look for new defenses. He is told: Your old equipment is unusable, your morality is a class product. History is your judge, you can't run away and hide from it. "If history is my judge," man then thinks, "if my heart is merely a reflection of my class interests, if my actions are worthless unless they are sanctioned by history, what is left me? My conscience? What good is my conscience, when it is others who will judge me anyway? All that is left me is my own nose and my own ears."

Words like this sound the alarm; such words are a great threat. The part of the silent puppet is the most unworthy part a man can play. We should eliminate such things from our lives. In building our reality we permitted the growth of utopias. One of the most insane of these tried to throw the concept of good will overboard and evaluate human conduct exclusively in the light of external consequences: "Your action is harmful, therefore you *wanted* to cause harm." Man fears such a judgment, capitulates before it; he senses that it does violence to his human nature, that it is extrahuman, if not inhuman. There is such a thing as humanity's bottom limit, below which one cannot descend. There are some experiments to which man should never be subjected. There is a pain that really crushes, there is a degree of fear that really freezes him. Man's capitulation under the impact of extreme situations is not subject to moral judgments; it can be described, but it cannot be judged. If he did not withstand extreme pain, this means merely that he did not withstand extreme pain, no more. One thing is certain: the human creature that can rely only on its nose and ears becomes more stupid than a chicken; it traces an ever narrowing circle around itself, and is afraid of crossing it. To develop the revolution we must free people from the magic chalk circles the Utopians have drawn.

One day during this period of ruthlessness I ran into Julka Glinska. It was one of those encounters that are impossible to forget. Her husband had not come back, she had no news of him. "He is innocent," she insisted. She had always known what he was thinking, and she was sure he could not have harmed the Party. She was one of those small but strong women who accept their share of misfortune calmly. She wanted to know the scope of the accusations against him, how long she would have to wait, how much strength she had to muster. She was completely in the dark—it was a new form, a new type of misfortune. I did not sense bitterness, even, in her voice, but there was something wrong about her eyes, and I heard a rumor that she had taken to drink. After she had been dismissed from the I.O.K., she had been unable to find a job and had grown thin and gaunt; only her former smiles remained.

"Richard's wife?" Piotr asked when, a few days later, I brought up the question of a vacancy in the Granada staff. Yes, she was Richard's wife. He had seen him at meetings of the underground organization in Filtrowa Street, before the outbreak of the Uprising. Piotr was sitting on the edge of a table, one leg on a chair. He had aged and grown gloomy in the course of the last few months. People were made uneasy by his silence, and when he spoke, it was in a low voice, without looking at the person he was addressing. "Tell her to come here tomorrow at ten," he murmured.

In the cafés, the Granada was the butt of many jokes. You must wear a dark suit for the opening, *Shock Brigade* will be the funeral of Art. At that time a new type of snob was being bred—a snob with leather patches on his elbows, a fashion of expropriated landowners which was now being adopted by expropriated humanists. They sat drinking black coffee with their consciences on their sleeves and their conflicts written all over their faces. These professional mourners initiated a silent boycott of the Granada. They walked about in a special way—with their heads stiff, as though carrying an invisible weight. "We are unsullied," their glances whispered; they would gladly have worn a placard with these words on their chests; their girl friends read Kafka's *The Trial* and pronounced it a work of genius.

Meanwhile an interesting development was taking place at the Granada: the company became converted to the text of the scorned play.

Later this was branded as a "loss of standards," but it was not as simple as that. The Granada company was made up of people. Aversion for pointless effort is a human characteristic. Once you put your hand to a job, it becomes precious to you; only those who stand aloof can remain skeptical. *Shock Brigade* grew more beautiful at each rehearsal, as the company saw their own efforts—the nights of discussion, the quarrels, the joy in solving specific problems—embodied in it. No one dared doubt any longer. They had imposed a rigorous rule on themselves: because the truth is in us, what we do is the truth.

Only on the night before the opening did they lose courage. They had but a few hours before them, and those hours could not change anything. They were seized with panic when they realized that everything was done; that people would come and judge them. Now that their work was ready, it became at once irrevocable and alien to them. How poor the finished product looked! After giving everything they had, they were as poor as beggars. The theater was filling up, and they had lumps in their throats. With dry lips they whispered their lines, and their heads swam with fright. Only the old actress who played the part of the Mother was calm. She spread out her solitaire deck in the dressing room. "Never live your part too much," she advised. "Routine is the best bet." A minute before the bell Rena Szulc rushed backstage, out of breath. She brought the latest news: Do you know who is in the first row? She listed the names of the people sitting in the first row. There were also miners in the house, who had come from a congress then being held in Warsaw. "Don't disappoint them," begged Rena Szulc. "Who let you in here?" Piotr asked softly. He was white with rage, and the others had to calm him down. Rena was gone. "Miners," he said through his clenched teeth. "So it's miners she's interested in, the whore . . ." At that moment the gong sounded.

A dimly-seen dense crowd, lights glaring in your eyes, applause, the shuffling of many feet after the curtain falls. Then the gong again, the rustle of pages in the prompter's booth, a missed cue, waves of heat emanating from the footlights, and more applause. Later they recalled it all like jumbled images in a feverish dream. Success! They had conquered the audience! The entire press was favorable. People came backstage to congratulate them, to shake their hands. For the three hours of the first performance, the company had again managed to identify themselves with the play. The fear that had momentarily all but thrown them off their feet, was swept away by the enthusiastic reviews. Hadn't they all been mentioned by name? And how many curtain calls had there been, exactly? And the young people? Hadn't the young given them an ovation?

For one week, for two, they lived as though on an isle of bliss; only echoes of praise reached them from the outside world. Nothing disturbed their victory. They forgave those who remained silent their envy; now they could afford to be magnanimous. The rapture lasted for a month, and they were full of love for the world. Then Swatkowski and Miernik came with a plan for "organizing the audience." The proposal was rejected with contempt: even if a few seats were empty, this merely meant that the public was slow to hear about the value of the play. But ten days later the plan was adopted; there were dark gaps in the audience, the house was half empty.

6.

"Try to understand what happened. Put yourself in our place and try to understand. Why didn't they want to come? Only the collective tickets sold. Why did we have to mobilize the high schools? Our heads burst with these questions. We continued to be congratulated, school girls presented us with flowers, blushing prettily. But if the unions and other institutions had not bought blocks of tickets, two thirds of the seats would have been empty. We knew it. Did you know that unsold seats creak of themselves? Yes, they creak of themselves. We were afraid of it. Why didn't people "from the city" come? We dragged on the performances by sheer will power. After one performance, the box office girl (yes, by then we had box office girls and doormen in green coats) said, 'Please, come and see for yourself.' Under a chair in the fourteenth row she had found an empty half-pint bottle of vodka and the remains of chicken legs. I gathered it all up and carried it out. The girl was nice, she didn't tell anyone else. And next day an elderly worker came backstage to thank us. 'I'll send my children,' he said. 'So they can see the play. After all, it's really for children.' I'm telling you, it's enough to drive us crazy."

That was Woynar, the youngest of the "three." He had a handsome delicate face, the alert eyes of David with the sling, and dark curly hair, which he combed with his fingers. His weapon, however, was not a sling. He had been a gunner, firing a mortar from the roof of the Power Plant during the Uprising. Later he had swum across the Vistula and contracted tuberculosis. He was a friend of Piotr's.

Everything he said was true. The universal comment on

Shock Brigade was: it's a good performance, the company has made an honest effort, it's worth seeing. And that was that. As though the adjectives "good," "honest," and "worthwhile" were not sufficient. All this led to a peculiar result: no one wanted to cross the ditch of favorable opinion. A fact had been recorded: the performance was good, honest, and worthwhile—there was no need to verify this fact for oneself. Isolated by this peculiar ditch, the company experienced a new kind of torment. Criticism! Why were there no criticisms? Insults would have been welcomed. Anything would have been preferable to this flattering indifference, this quicksand of encouraging clichés. The members of the company wanted to defend themselves, to give battle. But against whom? The adversary eluded them. How could they give battle on the swampy ground that now surrounded the Granada? They felt besieged, without hope of sortie, by an invisible enemy. They could only conclude that the enemy must lie inside, within themselves.

Twenty or so wounded people, young people who have been hurt and disillusioned, are a dangerous group. The world had seen many a defeat, this was not the first time an idea had capitulated. But this was different: no one attacked their idea, on the contrary, the authorities confirmed it, loudspeakers at street corners proclaimed it every hour. Were they to yield? Yield to whom? Were there any alternative arguments save those advanced by the mortal enemy of the revolution? The revolution, the Party, the People's Government—everything they had accepted as their own—stood by them, stood by their truth. If, a few months earlier, they had had doubts as to the purposefulness of their effort, they could no longer admit such doubts. They wanted to defend themselves. To defend themselves meant at present to defend the revolution. To it they had sacrificed the best they had; if this expense of energy had been wasted, they must have committed an error somewhere. This error, which accounted for the failure of their victory, must be discovered. Now, the causes of all errors invariably lie in people. The wounded group turned its eyes in on itself. A mercilessly keen eye began to probe each one of them.

Is there no flaw in your thinking? Isn't it possible that you are harboring a doubt whose mere presence undermines others? Do you remember our talk of a year ago? On that occasion you shrugged your shoulders twice. Why did you shrug your shoulders then? Kindly explain this today. If you want to be with us, we must make sure that our thinking is identical on every point. We cannot have different thoughts, they must coincide exactly. The slightest divergence opens a crack for the enemy. So, now, explain yourself, show what you are made of. But we warn you in advance: do not be different from us.

And what about you? You said once that you had some unsolved personal affairs. Aren't you dragging them along after you? You're dragging them as a runaway horse drags an axle tree that has parted company from the wagon, they knock you off your feet, it's enough to look at you. So you're that much of a weakling? Let us take a look at your personal history: your father was a bourgeois. You still haven't got rid of your class atavisms, you go about among us still carrying your bourgeois hump. I make you smile? That is a mistake on your part. Didn't you, by any chance, consider smuggling yourself abroad in 1945? True, you didn't go. But we don't know what you may be thinking today.

Don't you wear a mask? Yes, it's you I am talking about. You were always reluctant to condemn the adversary. Your appeals for mercy for the enemy, your respect for other people's beliefs, and your pity for the vanquished oblige us to draw certain inferences. They lead us to assume that you haven't fought hard enough against all that is foreign within yourself, and that some of your thoughts help and comfort the enemy. Now, don't interrupt, you'll have your chance to speak. Do you know that we call this double-dealing? You're quite right, we don't inhabit your soul, we can judge you only by your words and actions. And it is precisely your words and actions that, *objectively*, tend to blur class contradictions. Our word for that is: opportunism. Why are you silent? Convince us that we are mistaken, or else draw the logical conclusion from our reproaches. Certainly you cannot remain as you are.

They were merciless in posing such questions. They tormented each other with them. And in most cases the questions did not fail to reach the target. After all, they knew each other well enough for that. The less honest ones managed to wriggle out: they simply lied. The less courageous ones asked for time to make amends. But some were accursedly scrupulous, and every criticism led them to discover criminal traits and illicit desires in themselves. There are no errors whose causes cannot be discovered in people; but it is also true that there are no errors that an honest man cannot suspect himself of.

Swatkowski and Miernik declared that this soul-searching was "a desirable phenomenon." Taking the floor they stressed the importance of educational work in the company. "Our company is growing stronger, we can say that at last we are on the right path." They were listened to with a mingling of anxiety and hope. Nevertheless, their final conclusions stressed the necessity of a greater effort: "We are still a long way from having caught up with the work of construction; we lag behind reality." Such words, uttered with an obvious concern for impartiality, sounded solid and convincing; no one could doubt but that he lagged behind reality.

In his formal summations of the meetings, Piotr surpassed them all in cruelty. This boy with parched lips had for some time been going about saying the worst truths about everyone to his face. When he got up from his seat, it was always to wound, and his aim was deadly. "I will say everything right through to the end," he would say quietly. "Don't interrupt me, for it has to be said." The company trembled in anticipation of what would come out of Piotr's mouth, and they listened meekly in silence. He raked things up out of the remote past, he combed through the early years of each one of them, trying to lay bare the source of weakness. They had not dirtied *their* hands with the revolution, had they? They had been willing to have it given them ready made, they were quite ready to accept the fruits of victory in the class struggle. Did they have the slightest notion of what a revolution was? Could they grasp with their imaginations the blood and toil of the Russian proletariat during the years of the revolution? No little courage is required not to draw back before such a comparison. At the very first barricade, the first difficulty, you anxiously look at your hands, to see whether they have not been soiled. What enormous value you set upon yourselves! Yet when some blimp of the general staff sent you up against Tiger tanks, you didn't think your skins so precious. Even today you're ready to display your scars to the hucksters, and you are scared to death merely because the hucksters boycott the Granada. Silly fools! Do you think you can go through the revolution and keep your petty bourgeois shopkeeper's honor intact? Why, they would have hanged us from the first street lamp and laughed at our wounds. People like you are setting out to transform man? Do you expect to lift the old rock of the world from its foundation with those puny muscles? You'd do better to open a stall at the Rozycki Market, and peddle *Care* parcel stuff, instead of pretending to change the world. Let the Chinese coolies do the bleeding! Let the Korean peasants risk their lives for you, subtle intellectuals of the Granada!

They forgave him the hatred that made his voice shake, for they understood that he hated himself also, and that his accusations were also self-accusations. The shrewdest among them might have made use of their right to ask him questions, too: after all, Julka Glinska worked in the office of the Granada. But somehow they chose to spare Piotr, and never mentioned the one thing *he* kept to himself. Julka was adored by the girls in the box office, the doormen addressed her as "Comrade Julia." Everybody picked up the hairpins that she was always losing; her hair was always coming undone. Seeing Julka and Piotr together, the young men of the company wrinkled their foreheads and wondered; next day they would patiently listen to another of his speeches, which were by no means invariably fair to them. It was as though they had granted him some special rights.

But a few, without condemning Piotr, quietly debated with themselves whether they could stand the pressure. Secretly appealing to common sense, they asked themselves where it was all leading to, and to what extent this sort of thing was really necessary. The bolder ones asked for the floor, and put the question publicly.

"I can't stand it any longer," said Jacek Woynar. "I don't see why I must pay with my whole life for our having produced a bad play. What I wanted to found was a theater, not a hell. Rationalism is a feature of our revolution. You have brought things to such a point that I am afraid to think. When I do begin to think I reach the conclusion that I cannot think correctly because I am a lawyer's son. I have never been a mystic. I quit."

They wanted to expel him from the company, but Yust was opposed to this. "Very well, then, we'll talk with him," Piotr said. They talked for three successive meetings of the executive board. The matter was finally referred to the Doctor.

He had been informed about it, and received them at once. That was what he was there for—to detect and give special treatment to damaged souls. Whenever anyone began to doubt the usefulness of his existence in relation to higher and more necessary things—the Doctor, at the sight of such crises and depressions, displayed paternal satisfaction, and was ready to bestow on the poor soul his special smile of compassionate understanding. He was widely admired for this. But at the same time he was reproached for his contempt for humanity: "His impersonal approach may easily be taken for disinterestedness—it is the disinterestedness of the species performing its function. He does not see the individual man, he reacts only to the system of phenomena, within which man is a microorganism."

But it must be granted that he did not like to destroy people unnecessarily; he had, it was said, a "dialectical sense of eternity."

7.

In our city the crowd in the streets moves along broadened sidewalks, at the foot of buildings now higher than ever before. In a dull, painful restlessness this crowd is out to find the *taste* of the current day. Thirsting for sharp stimuli, it fills the movie houses, the stadiums, and the bars. Social motivations for existence do not satisfy it, although it was compelled to recognize their logic, supported daily by a thousand arguments. Generally speaking, arguments convince it, for the crowd is not insane; it grasps the importance of work in its life, it does not underestimate the need for the organization of individual efforts, it respects physical energy, which is to be the source of future achievements. But all this does not dispel anxiety. Principles and goals do not exhaust its longings. Tormented by obscure needs, craving to forget the program of its accomplishments, it seeks the taste of life, which would enable it to feel pleasure in immediate existence. In this, it is not choosy—it takes what is given. Alcohol provides the surest guarantee of reconciliation with the present: a pint bottle of vodka contains just the right percentage of irrationality. "He has given himself spirit," we Poles say of a drunk, or "He's gassed up." "Gas" is the spirit of our era. At night, jets flying at speeds faster than sound pass over the heads of the drunks. Some little man, precision instruments the only thing between him and nothingness, will step out of a silvery cigar—perhaps in our lifetime—onto one of the stars. No epoch has fulfilled so many eternal human dreams as the twentieth century will fulfill. Despite all that, man at mid-century is more than ever devoured by restless boredom, and never before has he been separated from his victories by so many things. Between ourselves and that which we are capable of, there yawns an incomprehensible abyss; it is as though we had outstripped ourselves. So long as that gap remains unfilled, so long as the revolution has not made it a territory accessible to man, so long as man has not learned to use and control it, he is doomed to the desperate anxiety of a being that does not know its destiny, that remains subject to obscure and irrational forces So long as this is true, he has not yet attained freedom.

"You are free," the West is told by its spokesmen, "we spread before you a marvelous world of nylon and plastics, masterpieces of comfort, neons in all colors, women with the most beautiful bodies, the subtlest play of lights and the fastest pace. You are free, we give you the taste of life, not for nothing to be sure, but of the very best quality. We give you everything you need to keep from being devoured by the restless pain of existence, so that you may drown out all thought of goal and principle in yourselves. Do not look for a social motivation for existence, because you will find only strife and anxiety." Such a state of affairs, which is in a sense the reverse of ours, is not satisfactory in the long run: ignorance of the goal, and sense of the alogicality of existence produce hunger for a program, longing for a new order of thought, a surfeit with publicity, a shortage of ideas. Dazed by the pace and the brilliance, stimulated by narcotics, corroded by the "spleen" of civilization—man in that part of the world does not understand the formula of his life, does not know whither he is going, enjoys only the semblance of freedom.

Let us keep in mind both the one and the other profile of modern man, who wants to be the free possessor of the new capacities conquered by mankind. Only too often has mankind been told that one must wear chains in order to be free, and be blind in order to see the truth.

If, blindfolded and trusting, you run into a wall, don't open your eyes, you are told, this is a wall of enemy forces, you must break through it; if you feel weak, this means that the wall is also within you. And so, close ranks! Forward, march!

The Granada company tried to make a tiny breach in the invisible wall separating it from freedom. Slawski, Woynar and Yust really loved freedom. They knew that in their century freedom is born of revolution. There was no need for strenuous persuasion to make them understand their age, to make them forgive it its cruelties. Slawski, Woynar, Yust and their comrades were of a generation that eagerly looks forward. Thirsting for the meaning of the present, they entrusted themselves to it unconditionally, and postponed till some later time, some time after victory, the job of dealing with what is still bad in it. Do not smile ironically—no generation is free of such mistakes. Moreover it was not easy to find one's way during the unsettled postwar years. Are we wiser today than they were? We may think that we are, but tomorrow or the day after tomorrow, those 1940s and 1950s may amaze us by the immensity of the things that were accomplished.

But let us return to the Granada, to the torment of those who doubted, and not without reasons; to the others, the unmoved ones, who broke down the doubters, and whom we denounce today with a shame and anger all the greater because we have waited so long before speaking up.

I do not know what happened during the talk between Jacek Woynar and the Doctor; I only know its consequences. After that talk, Woynar became silent and compliant. He did not repeat his rebellious outbursts, he voted along with the others, and rarely asked for the floor. Occasionally a smile was to be seen on his lips. Those who thought they knew him well insisted that he had not smiled like that before. This was something new; some speakers angrily averted their eyes when they saw that smile, others lost the thread of an idea they had begun to advance. Someone even hinted that Woynar should be questioned. But what about? About his smile? What kind of organizational business is a smile? It was all the more troubling because Woynar could not be reproached with anything else. He did not stalk out of meetings, he performed all his duties. He began to comb his hair, and to dress more carefully. Swatkowski and Miernik said that Woynar had passed through an ideological crisis and come out on the right road. Rena Szulc spread this news far and wide.

8.

The hundredth performance of *Shock Brigade* was approaching. The play continued sluggishly, but continued. In rehearsal were two one-act plays by Fredro; it had been planned to act them in modern dress, but Swatkowski and Miernik shook their heads: such a thing would be an experiment, and we could not afford experiments, they said, with a working class audience. Therefore, hoop skirts, lace ruffles and other paraphernalia were ordered; their cost would be covered by the Institute. The Institute would also pay for a banquet after the hundredth performance; important guests were invited, the press would carry articles and interviews, and workers from the Zeran plant would attend the hundredth performance in a body.

On that solemn day, Stanislaw Zaczynski, the doorman of the Granada Theater, turned on the lights in the lobby at four P.M. He turned on the lights, then lit a cigarette, and glanced into the box office—the girl was due at any moment. Zaczynski's brother worked on the MDM building project, and the doorman had promised to give him a free ticket for today; the brothers had agreed to meet at four o'clock in front of the ticket window. A few minutes later the brother, Leon, entered the lobby in a quilted jacket smeared with white dust, shuffling his rubber boots. "We'll have to wait," Zaczynski said, "the cashier hasn't got here yet." He began to sweep out the lobby, casting an occasional glance at Leon, who was looking at the poster for the hundredth performance. "Hey, are they playing something different today?" the younger brother whispered after a moment. "What do you mean?" said Zaczynski. "It's the *Brigade*, the hundredth time." "It says something else here," Leon said, laughing, and pointed to the poster. It said: *The Bath*.

Zaczynski said nothing, but put down his broom. On the wall next to the ticket window was a poster with a large red caption. Most of its surface was filled with the face of a man with short-cropped hair. This man was looking angrily into Zaczynski's eyes. Below this face was lettering, as though someone had clumsily splashed red ink on the poster. *The Bath*—Zaczynski read. And Leon pointed his grimy finger at another inscription, running diagonally across the man's mouth—a strip of paper pasted over the poster with black lettering said: CENSORED.

"Censored?" the younger Zaczynski was surprised. "Then why did they post it?" But the expression on his brother's face silenced him. They stood there for quite a while, unable to take their eyes off the oddly familiar face of the young man, who seemed to be trying to tell them something important.

If I remember correctly, it was at that banquet after the hundredth performance that Piotr's name began to be linked with Julka Glinska's. Her husband had still not got out of prison. People know everything, nothing can remain hidden from human eyes. Who was the first to discover their case? Not "love," but "case," for what took place between them provided material for so many accusations and depositions, that one can without irony compare it to public proceedings in a jammed courtroom. A certain critic once wrote that in our age "love is not a focal point of social problems," that we live in a virile period of struggle. I suppose the critic was right, yet even in our age love can explode with maximum force and shattering consequences. What is to be done then? The critic will be of no help. In all epochs there is a prohibited, desperate, hopeless love; a love that others destroy. Who was the first to keep track of her every word and act? For this was what now began to occur daily. People passed on the exact words Piotr had used when he spoke to Julka, only a few days before the banquet. Their conversation was supposed to have taken place in the theater office, separated from the ticket booth only by a thin partition. Was it the girl at the box office, then? Or had someone merely dropped by just in time to hear Piotr say, "You are not to go back to him, you are going to live with me. Can you take back a confirmed traitor? If you will not have me, at least tell me why. I want to know why."

Today, several years later, I know many persons who look upon these words as "another proof" of Piotr's baseness. On such occasions I feel a sudden pain. Yesterday's guardians of the most cruel abstractions are still among us, and are ready, as always, to hurl accusations. To display their newly-acquired righteousness they must step on helpless people, and by crushing them underfoot climb up themselves. Part of the truth they certainly know—no question about it—but how skillfully they use it, how cleverly they put up the prices on the commodity market, those little brokers on the stock exchange of dialectics, with their nose for ups and downs, the rising and falling values of the class struggle! And what terrible damage they can do, once they get hold of a particle of truth, all they need to start operating and speculating. It is humiliating to have to defend certain things and people against them. I suppose Piotr did say those words, cruel and blind as they were: he was consistent to the end, and if he believed in that man's crime, he could judge him only as a criminal. But had he been convinced of the man's innocence, the same Piotr Slawski would not have hesitated a moment . . . Some of those who today quote his words as proof of his villainy, at that time—three or four years ago—blamed him for committing a political crime. Then, they had not said, "It is ignoble to stab a helpless man in the back," but: "He is corrupt through and through, a Party member should not associate with the wife of a counter-revolutionary." The critic was right: love is not a theme for our epoch. The theme of our epoch is the struggle against the bourgeois.

The moment a relationship between two persons falls into the hands of strangers, it ceases to be love. People do not condemn lovers; they merely subject their union to the corrosive action of social acids. Each era has its laboratory for treating love with current reagents; as a rule the lovers emerge from it transmuted. Julka and Piotr had to overcome many small obstacles, and one great obstacle exceeding human strength. Before Piotr could realize how much he was asking, before he was able to grasp the truly great obstacle to their love, an obstacle that actually did exist, several smaller obstacles, raised by strangers' hands, began to appear.

The first was erected by Swatkowski and Miernik. On the day of the hundredth performance of *Shock Brigade*, some unknown hand had posted in the outer lobby the poster for *The Bath*, which had been printed the preceding fall, in anticipation of the opening that never took place. Diagonally across the poster, across the poet's mouth, a malicious hand had scrawled the jeering inscription. The doorman Zaczynski tore it down and took it to the office. Although the subsequent investigation was carried out with the utmost discretion, the culprit remained undetected. Swatkowski and Miernik, responsible for the political purity of the company, began to study their files, to summon individuals for private conferences, to go over the fabric of each man's past with the delicacy of a weaver in reverse, taking his handiwork apart. Finally they undertook a real purge of the personnel. Those who were submissive were treated with charity—for they could still be of use. Swatkowski and Miernik adhered to the theory of "soft bodies": according to this theory, a soft body is the best building material. The harder bodies, consequently, were treated according to the principle of the Holy Inquisition—"Kill them all—God will recognize His own!" Among those fired from their jobs was Julka Glinska.

Piotr was at that time away from Warsaw. When he came back, a few days later, she was not in the office where he expected to find her. Everyone was afraid to tell him what had happened. "Listen, we watched him go looking for her," Jacek Woynar told me later. He went over the entire building and opened every door. He was as afraid to ask as we were to tell him. For the first time Piotr was afraid of something. "Piotr — can you believe it! In the end, Olek Yust told him."

Piotr took it calmly enough. That same day Swatkowski and Miernik informed him that the Doctor wanted to see him. And so he drove to the Institute to give the man behind the desk the last thing he possessed.

9.

Several years separate us from the events I am describing. Today, time throws no mantle of obscurity over human affairs, it drags them out from the darkness: an ever larger number of previously unnoticed dramas appear in broad daylight. So it was in this case. No one died, no one was buried under "the dust of oblivion," and all the people of the Granada are alive today. True, many of them changed during those years; that was a period of radical transformations, and I often hear the opinion expressed that a man today is worth only as much as he went through during those years. Each of us still carries a heavy burden from that period, and when anyone throws his down with a shrug of his shoulders, the burden merely falls on others.

Not long ago I ran into the doorman of the Granada on the suburban train to Otwock. Zaczynski recognized me, even though I had not stopped at the theater in Polna Street for over a year. We filled the short trip with talk—it is not hard to guess what about. Shortly before we pulled into Otwock, Zaczynski was silent for a few moments, then asked if I knew what had become of Piotr. I repeated to him what I had been told. The doorman nodded. "That was a man, Mr. Editor," he said. "That was a man. And why did I have to show them the poster, will you tell me that? I helped. Everyone had a hand in this misfortune, Mr. Editor. I suppose it had to be that way."

The case of Julka and Piotr dragged on for several more months. It could not be ended by one talk with the Doctor. Even a talk between themselves could not have ended it. They lacked strength. The destruction of love requires a longer time, they were destroying theirs only with difficulty. A tree is cut down all at once, but love is brought down more slowly.

They were seen together a few more times at a dirty little café on the outskirts of Warsaw. Bent over a table, they spoke in whispers, unsmilingly, or remained silent for minutes at a time. It was the end of the winter, an unexpectedly snowy one. Warsaw is a small city, there are no streets where one never sees a familiar face. Every time the door opened, the woman sitting at the corner table looked up. It was later reported (but, for heaven's sake, how could people know this?) that Piotr was now interested in only one thing. He demanded that Julka tell him the truth: was Richard a traitor? He tormented her with questions, asking her to recall the smallest details of her conversations with him, to recreate in its entirety one or another day during the occupation—whom had he run into in the street, who had come to see him? "This is the most important thing to me," Piotr would say, "whether or not he was guilty. This will decide everything." He swore to her that he would not repeat what she told him to anyone, that he would keep the truth to himself; he would share it only with her, for he could not live without her, she was crucial to him. "Don't torment me," she would beg. "What can I say except that Richard is innocent? You demand the truth of me, and what about me? It is I who should be demanding, screaming for the truth. Do you think I don't know how many shameful lies are being circulated about him?" Then he would begin again from the beginning: had she never had any suspicions? Was it not possible that he had kept everything secret even from her? Could she know all his contacts? . . . He asked maniacal questions, and did not seem to hear her appeals. Such was the dialogue of their love affair that had begun at the theater in Polna Street.

During the next three years I lost all contact with the Granada. I read notices and reviews of new productions in the newspapers. The Granada was one of the few theaters that could boast of real achievements. In 1952 the company received a government award for its production of *Engineer Marek*, a play by a Czech author. The press emphasized the honesty of the effort and the valuable work done. It deplored only the absence of references to Polish problems. The universal weak point of contemporary theaters.

Piotr was no longer directing the company. "He had reached the end of his rope," it was said. "He worked less and less well." For quite some time Yust had been carrying out the functions of director, Olek Yust, as patient as a camel, certainly the most sensible of the "three." Without his stubbornness the company would have disintegrated. He was one of those unobtrusive people, who rarely push themselves forward, but whose true worth is revealed when things go badly. His voice was reassuring. In *The Bath* he was to have played the part of the Author. Tall, blond, he moved his great arms with careful restraint, and was often seen with a petite student at the School of Plastic Arts. They were married last year.

Actually the theater was directed by Swatkowski and Miernik. The administrative staff was increased, the department for "organization of the audience" occupied three rooms, and the figures on fulfilled quotas were displayed on the walls. During that time the Granada company had changed in composition. Some people had left, others came in, often from the provinces. The Granada had become more serious—the members were less disheveled, they wore Polish-made coats. Basically nothing had happened, everything went on as before, the thing "played itself." Only a few searching observers maintained that the Granada had capitulated. To whom? That was the question! To no one, to the forces of anonymity. They had stopped fighting, it was said, because for the enemy they had substituted a *concept*. What can you fight for, if reality is no more than the sum of proved assumptions? At first they had staged plays, now they were a department of the I.O.K. "Look at them! The only thing that really interests them is avoiding mistakes. And to avoid mistakes, why, this is the professional concern of bookkeepers. Why single themselves out by pretending they are a theatrical company?"

As for Piotr, his fall was variously commented on. The preponderant view was that he had collapsed after breaking with Julka Glinska. If this was true, then his subsequent visits to the Doctor's office take on a strange eloquence. For it was the Doctor who had demanded of Piotr that he "clean up his life"—and once he had done so, what was the purpose of his continuing visits? During the period of these visits he lost interest in the theater. Allegedly (just how is difficult to understand, yet details of these talks were known in town) Piotr insisted that the Doctor give him an explanation of the case of Richard Glinski. Had it really been proved that he worked for a foreign agent? That he had committed treason? Allegedly (once again, "allegedly") Piotr would leave the Doctor's office convinced—only to come back three weeks later to ask for fifteen minutes of the Doctor's time, to reopen the Glinska case from the beginning, and once again to leave the office reassured. He had grown thin and cadaverous. There were complaints about him at the theater: he walked out of meetings, did not treat the actors properly.

"He's in the spotlight," some said, "and can't get out of it."

You can explain everything with a metaphor: nothing is easier than to compare a man to a hare, a fox, or an ant. What concerned Piotr, I suppose, was his last chance: he wanted to know whether what had been done with him was necessary. Everything had been taken away from him, he had nothing left. What he still wanted to know was whether that "nothing" which had been left was any good to anyone at all. He had given everything away to confirm himself, his rightness. And yet this was not enough, for the truth had not been proved. For Piotr the problem of truth was somehow tied up with Richard's case. He could think of nothing else. He had probably come to believe that the "traitor" must have been "one of them," he or Richard. Yes, I think he reached this conclusion, that one of them was a traitor, and that one of them must bear the final consequences. He went to the Doctor for proof of the truth. Some truths can be proved by the testimony of witnesses; but there are other truths whose proof demands victims.

At the time I preferred not to think about it. Many of us had their Granadas and Doctor Fauls in those years. I had some of my own.

Toward the end of last year I had a letter from Julka. She wrote that Richard had been released from prison, and the charges against him dropped. Then she added a P.S.: "There was a terrible thing involving Piotr. Don't try to find out any more. He was saved."

10.

"I was the first to discover him. I had promised to lend him a book, and that day I brought it to him. I came at almost the last moment. You will find it hard to believe, but I was not surprised. During those years nothing could surprise me any more. Do you recall that after I had spoken against *Shock Brigade* I had a talk with the Doctor? He didn't convince me then. That was the first time he failed to convince me—and he knew it. I walked out of his office with my legs shaking, for I realized that from then on I'd be alone, and the thought frightened me . . . Everything became hideously clear. I sat at the meetings listening to Piotr, and I had to hold myself back from walking up to him and asking him: Why are you talking like this? Why do you throw dust in our eyes and yours? Look behind you: don't you see a petty bourgeois standing there, terrified that the crowd is going to pillage his little hoard of abstractions? . . . Piotr wanted to believe to the bitter end, and I knew that he at least was incapable of lying; but the others—so it seemed to me—all the others were lying. I sat still, I voted with the majority. I no longer worried about where we were all headed, I was only interested in the causes for it all. I watched closely, trying to discover *how* it was all happening. At the time I wouldn't have told you this, I preferred to remain silent. I'm telling it to you only today, in 1955, and I may as well admit that even today I don't understand it all. What was it? Any toady nowadays thinks himself cleverer than we were in those years. You must hear them talking, too, the stuffed shirts who are boasting everywhere, "We weren't taken in." Nowadays any kind of conscience suffices any kind of scoundrel. And yet we believed in those years. How did it come about that, although we didn't lie, we did not at the same time tell the truth? Tell me—I can't find the answer . . .

"Do you know whom Piotr bumped into two days before I brought him the book and had to break down his door? He had run into Richard Glinski. At that time no one knew that he had been released. Piotr was walking along the street, and there, all of a sudden, was Richard. Julka told me about it a week later. They went to a bar and stayed there for three hours. For the first time in five years they had an opportunity to talk about the revolution. Do you understand now? He had met in the street a man whom he had looked upon as a traitor for five years; he had to listen to his story for three hours, for three hours he had to feel his eyes resting on him— knowing and remembering the thing the other could not yet have known. Piotr was the strongest of us all, but he was not strong enough to endure that. So now you understand? . . . I don't know how the Doctor reacted to the incident. Just then he was particularly busy, and when Olek Yust would ring him up, the secretary always said that the Doctor was in conference. Swatkowski and Miernik were also attending some conference or other, they were all devilishly busy! But the news got around, and there were many who saw to it that it spread everywhere. A filthy rumor began to circulate in the city. Scandal at the Granada! Now, everybody could get his dirty hands on us. Do you know who were the first to appear on the scene? The boys with the patches on their elbows. No, I forgot, they weren't wearing leather patches any more—instead they had all grown little beards. They began to come around, with sympathetic faces, as considerate and polite as ever. They had grown beards because that was the fashion, but it looked as though they had grown them in secret. They addressed everyone as 'Mister': 'Mr. So-and-so, do you know how Mr. Slawski is doing? Even though we had many differences, we believe in fair play, and we think this is the proper time for us to understand each other without all those phrases, which, after all, you yourselves, gentlemen, never believed.'

"You get it, don't you? 'We know that you were forced to lie, you were cynics for sensible reasons, and even though we weren't taken in, we are the first to hold out our hands to you—now when a new wind is about to blow away that mysterious fog which you called your ideology.' I hadn't been so disgusted for a long time . . . They looked at us with encouraging grief in their eyes: We'll forgive everything, dear, beloved swine, if you will only weep on our bosoms. Let's have a good cry together—we, the unsullied ones, and you, who were deep in the mud, let us shed tears together over the grave of the revolution . . . A few weeks later, when Piotr was out of the hospital, Yust and I took him to a country house in the Mazury. He was still weak, and had to lie down in the railway compartment. We didn't know whether he was asleep or had just closed his eyes. And I was continually haunted by the fear that we were not accompanying Piotr, but only his dead body. 'His and ours, Olek,' I thought looking at Yust, 'for he had taken on his own shoulders the burden that ought to have weighed equally on us all.' "

This was in the spring, at the old Five Ponds home; the man speaking was Jacek Woynar.

*

The rest—if it can be called "the rest"—I learned from Yust several months later. That day, on the corner of Foksal Street and Nowy Swiat, when he solemnly informed me of Thomas Mann's death, I did not let him get away. He was in a hurry to get to a rehearsal at the Granada. What rehearsal? He refused to tell me, but if I had time, he said, I could go with him. I should see, yes, it wouldn't be a bad idea if I went with him to Polna Street. It was a hot day. We dragged ourselves sluggishly in the direction of the theater.

"You haven't been there for a long time," said Yust, "you don't know all that's been going on. No, Piotr hasn't come back yet. He is director of a Community Hall near Olsztyn. He has recovered, completely recovered. He wants to stay there through the winter."

He wanted to stay there for the winter, although they had gone to see him and also wrote begging him to come back. They needed him again. How had all this come about? That is what everyone wanted to know. Yust would not reply to questions of this kind. Did I know that Richard had been released? So I did know certain things, although I had not been to see them for so long.

We walked along the Aleje on the side that is occupied by government buildings and lined with tall trees. They gave a pleasant shade that scorching September day. The Doctor? . . . Yust had not seen him for a long time. The Doctor had recently given an interesting lecture on Thomas Mann, and he was organizing a chain of village theaters. His time is as precious as gold, but it must be admitted that he doesn't keep it for himself. This man, thin as a stick, nevertheless has the strength of a horse. They say he keeps up his studies; when? no one quite knows, probably at night. At the memorial meeting in honor of Thomas Mann, he astonished the audience with his profound knowledge of German literature. He had spoken for an hour and a half. He could always hold your attention despite a wooden voice, that much must be granted him. What were we to think of him? . . . Yust shrugged his shoulders. Doctor Faul—everybody now called him Doctor Faul—had become the living symbol of all our errors. But what was one really to think of him? Yust was walking slowly, taking long steps, making the gravel crunch under his rubber soles.

After taking Piotr to the country, and coming back to Warsaw, he and Woynar did not know what to do. The company! They had to hold the company together. How could they save the hard core of the Granada, which had been torn open, made to expose its wounds, and become the meat of a juicy scandal? Questions came at them from all sides: What is going to happen now? Is it true that we'll be disbanded? Is it true that the Granada can't be used at the present time for political reasons? It is true? All those years have been wasted? Woynar, Yust—tell us what has happened! Nobody wants to talk to us, people turn aside when they see us coming, the company is going to pieces. And the little beards! We hear our own thoughts of three years ago, our own doubts— but out of whose mouths? Have you see what the papers have been saying in the past few weeks? . . . Here, read what they write about the Granada!

The same people were still writing about the Granada— the same critics who had been favorable three years before. During the interval they had not changed their names or their methods. While formerly they declared with moderate emphasis that the Polna Street theater had achieved a break-through with respect to content (though at the price of some simplifications in form), now they pointed with moderate emphasis to inadmissible artistic crudities which (despite certain ideological achievements) had resulted in the falsification of reality. The same cautious, insipid smile, formerly tearful, now compassionate; the same impassable ditch; half-words and half-reproaches, painfully raised eyebrows, maliciously squinting eyes. A new period. Where is the adversary? Where is the enemy in this new period?

The Granada company was once again wounded and disillusioned, as it had been four or five years before, and as before was passionately though belatedly in search of the causes. It now began to look for the enemy within its own ranks. "Didn't you say that such and such a scene should be cut because its effect might prove harmful? Who has given you the right to be so sure of yourself? Why did you worry so about individual lines, when the overall meaning of the play was clear? . . . And you? Now you're quiet, but then you quoted authorities against us; but we could have quoted the same authorities against you . . . You were too scared, you didn't trust the masses, you tried to lock the anger of the proletariat in your drawers and filing cabinets . . . I? I wasn't like that, at least I was worried that we were moving in a false direction; but I kept quiet because of the others . . ."

Echoes of these quarrels spread far and wide. More and more strangers with friendly faces hovered ever more closely about the Granada ("it was as if they were standing in front of the theater," Yust said, "waiting for those who would go out banging the door"). Patiently glancing at their watches, they counted the time remaining till the end of Socialism; the idea would live only a few hours longer, and then its victims would celebrate its fall, and everyone would be invited to the feast.

Then, one day, Swatkowski and Miernik came in their green hats.

That day both wore them openly for the first time. "If you had seen them then, if you had seen those hats of smooth green felt, if you had seen how they were wearing them—oh, you wouldn't have laughed!" It was clear: this must have meant something, heads like those are not covered by accident. Rena Szulc came with them. You know Rena Szulc, perspiringly in search of next week's truths. Rena had tears in her eyes when she said: "We were out of touch with the people." That was on a Saturday. On Monday people began to say that the Granada in Polna Street would shortly become a theater for musical comedy.

The next day Yust and Woynar asked to see the Doctor. He received them. He sat behind the same desk; the calendar, the freshly sharpened pencils, the cold, attentive gleam of his glasses, all were the same. They must not imagine that they had taken him by surprise. If anyone was amazed, it was they, not the other way round. But he listened to the end. Yes, to the end: they brought up everything, they demanded an accounting of the past. Yust could not tell me, later, what he said on that occasion, or what Woynar said. Both felt constricted, they choked, stammered, could barely control themselves. "Do you know what he told us in answer? Can you guess what we were told by the man whose voice for years had guided our thoughts and judged our actions?"

"You have come to ask for an accounting. You want me to apologize. You hold me responsible for the evil inherent in those years. You have come here in the name of the revolution, to investigate my files and audit my ledgers. You have come on a day when the revolution is making a new effort— to know itself. You are wiser in consequence of that day and that effort. But have you stopped to think in the name of what I was speaking all these years? Surely in the name of my experience. Who can tell whether I was not compelled to pass on to you my experience, which goes somewhat further back than yours? What did you know about the revolution when you were founding the Granada? An armored car with a red flag and a placard with the inscription, 'Leftward, march!' As it turned out, this scarcely exhausts the image of the revolution. The strength of the revolution is infinitely great. The forces of the revolution are so powerful that in some periods the revolution itself seems unable to endure them; then the world has the impression that we are destroying ourselves, that we are suppressing and limiting the revolution, by subjecting it to a hierarchy and a system. I am not justifying errors, but explaining them. I am not whitewashing myself, I merely wish to point out that the sacrifices I demanded of you—well, perhaps I had to demand them of myself, too. Am I responsible for the evil that was done? Yes, I am. But do not think that you are not. What I handed down to you, you handed down to others. You passed on to others your experience—the good and the evil that cannot be separated from each other in the revolution as easily as the meat is separated from the bones on a bourgeois table. That, to put it briefly, is our common truth."

That, to put it briefly, is what the Doctor replied to them. They listened to him, and just like five years ago, they fell silent. But this time they did not want to prolong the conversation with the Doctor, to repeat the bad dialogues of the past years. "We have no time," Yust said, "the truth is now ahead of us."

What have they decided? "You'll know in a moment," Yust said. "No, those years haven't been wasted. No years are ever wasted. Listen," he said, walking a little faster. "What we wanted to do five years ago, we'll do today, and do better." So the truth is ahead of them, and perhaps the future will solve the riddles that the various Doctors set them, but they must make up for lost time. Now they must be pure. Never before had they felt as closely united as they did now. Yust gave me his word for it. If only Piotr would come back.

They had dug the old copy of *The Bath* out of a drawer. They began to read it again; once again, the play passed from hand to hand. They read it somewhat differently than five years earlier. In the interval, they had earned the right to understand certain words. The tattered old copy brought them back to their own thoughts. Without previous agreement, they reached the unanimous conclusion that they had to start rehearsals again. Because some men had left, and others had come, the play was cast somewhat differently.

All this they undertook at their own risk, the truth was ahead of them and depended on them. Swatkowski and Miernik were informed of the company's decision: the company would not give up the Granada so that it could become a musical comedy theater. Rehearsals for *The Bath* had been going on for a week.

*

As so many times before I found myself once again in a small half-dark auditorium. The rehearsal was about to begin. The Author, as formerly, was to be played by Yust. The last of the house lights went out. In a moment, a man with angry eyes will appear on stage, a giant, whose foot has crushed the bourgeois beneath it. He will talk to us, he will speak with a full voice, thunderingly, assuring us that the train of the revolution has not yet stopped, that the fireman is not asleep, that the pistons of the red locomotive are still carrying it forward, skipping decades of history . . . The Granada company made its sacrifice to the revolution. How many of them are left? Ten, seven, three? If one of them survives, he alone will convince twenty more. Out of that twenty perhaps only three will hold out to the end, be strong enough to resist the pressure from all sides. And if out of those three, only one survives, he will try again. For they know that after the greatest losses there always remains a thing greater than any of them —a thing that is continually reborn and is never lost.

In a moment the Author will appear on stage.

"Curtain," someone cried. "Curtain going up!"

WARSAW, SEPTEMBER-OCTOBER 1955

Translated by Norbert Guterman

Zbigniew Herbert

The Philosophers' Den

PROLOGUE

(Music. Against a background of drums and brass—the shrieking of a whistle. The stage is empty and without scenery. The Chorus enters, dressed in short, light-colored skirts. Their faces are heavily made-up and they are wearing steep paper hats.)

FIRST MEMBER (bows deeply): Ladies and gentlemen, this whole thing is about Socrates, son of a midwife and a stone-cutter.

SECOND MEMBER: It's a story with a kernel.

THIRD MEMBER: Full of words, allusions and pauses.

FOURTH MEMBER: But unfortunately no action.

FIFTH MEMBER: Those who forgot to bring food can still escape.

SIXTH MEMBER: They will get their money back.

FIRST MEMBER: The play, as we said, is about a philosopher . . .

SECOND MEMBER: Who lived long . . .

THIRD MEMBER: Was active in the field of education . . .

FOURTH MEMBER: And didn't die a natural death.

FIFTH MEMBER: This surely adds spice to the matter . . .

SIXTH MEMBER: And a pinch of heroism.

FIRST MEMBER: You will have to use all your powers of perception . . .

SECOND MEMBER: To untie this knot . . .

THIRD MEMBER: Of lofty lies and shallow hypotheses.

FOURTH MEMBER: So we'll have to see with the eyes of others.

FIFTH MEMBER: There will be something here for both the shortsighted and the farsighted.

SIXTH MEMBER: But very little for those who can see well.

FIRST MEMBER: The author has asked us to give you his apologies because he won't provide the answer.

SECOND MEMBER: He says he doesn't have it.

THIRD MEMBER: He says that if he did have it he would have written the play in German.

FOURTH MEMBER: In which case, he wouldn't have had to bring the actors here and pull strings.

FIFTH MEMBER: Oh well, the point is, he doesn't have it.

SIXTH MEMBER: And we, who have mastered the art of acquiescence, must accept the fact.

FIRST MEMBER: Our attitude is justified, if only because the art goes back to ancient times.

SECOND MEMBER: When the technique of interrogation was poor.

THIRD MEMBER: For it was Socrates who first invented dialectics.

FOURTH MEMBER: The textbook on dialectics for interrogating judges was prepared much later.

FIFTH MEMBER: That's why the accused could indulge in his criminal activity for so long a period.

SIXTH MEMBER: And why his head, tossed on the high shore of our times, has such blurred features.

FIRST MEMBER: We will not play this sort of trick on our descendants.

SECOND MEMBER: All those sent to the other side will have stones tied to their necks with inscriptions of the paragraphs by which they died.

THIRD MEMBER: All other data will be destroyed so as not to tempt the psychologists.

FOURTH MEMBER: Those few who are innocent and infallible, we will embalm. Their works will also be embalmed and exhibited to the crowds free of charge.

FIFTH MEMBER: Thus mankind will be freed of dramas and art born of doubt. (*A whiplash is heard.*)

ALL: Let's begin.

ACT I

Scene 1

(*A stone prison. Twilight. On the bunk sits a man in an overcoat. To the left—a staircase; above it, a small window. The Council's Envoy and the Guard enter.*)

ENVOY: Is he asleep?

GUARD: Yes. He sleeps day and night.

ENVOY: Is he ill?

GUARD: No. He says he's simply getting used to death. An eccentric, you know.

ENVOY: Wake him up.

GUARD: Yesterday he asked me to leave him alone. People come here constantly and bother him. Are you one of his disciples?

ENVOY: No. I'm here in an official capacity.

GUARD: Ah, that's different. (*He shakes the sleeping man's shoulder.*) Hey, mister! Come back from the dark land of dreams to this barren, stony earth. Hey, I'm calling you! (*The man wakes, drops his legs over the side of the bunk and rubs his eyes. The Guard laughs.*)

ENVOY: I've come to see you, Socrates.

SOCRATES: So I see.

ENVOY: Did I disturb your dream?

SOCRATES: Yes.

ENVOY: What were you dreaming about?

SOCRATES: Nothingness—the soft, soothing element.

ENVOY: I understand, something like the sea. Do you recognize me?

SOCRATES: No.

ENVOY: I'm the Council's Envoy. I'm here on a mission. (*He signals the Guard to leave them alone.*)

Scene 2

ENVOY: As you know, the ship from Delos will arrive the day after tomorrow. This means that the day after tomorrow you will die. You understand, of course, that we've revived that old religious custom only to make your escape easier.

SOCRATES: Of course.

ENVOY: The Council is worried because you're so sluggish. What, in heaven's name, do you think you are doing?

SOCRATES: I'm content here, that's all. Before, I had to walk up and down the streets and my lectures were, so to speak, an outcome of chance. They were—to be precise—a collection of more or less witty aphorisms. Thanks to you, I will now create something worthy of respect—a system.

ENVOY: Please stop joking. People in the city are talking about your latest lecture on law. They say it was brilliant, but very reactionary.

SOCRATES: My, my.

ENVOY: Apparently, you advanced the thesis that laws must be obeyed.

SOCRATES: Yes.

ENVOY: Even when they're cruel?

SOCRATES: Even when they're cruel.

ENVOY: I'm a plain clerk, Socrates, and I would like to get to the bottom of this. The whole thing seems queer to me.

SOCRATES: No doubt it is.

ENVOY: Please don't interrupt me when I'm speaking. Just answer yes or no. The Phoenician merchants tell us that, in the deep interior of Africa, there are tribes which demand human sacrifices. This is one of their laws. And the Lacedaemonian law says that sickly children must be put to death. What do you say about that?

SOCRATES: *(remains silent.)*

ENVOY: Suppose that a tyrant suddenly appeared among us and issued an order saying that all adult Athenians must have their right arms cut off—what would you say about those Athenians who carried out the order? You'd probably say that they had stooped to the level of slaves.

SOCRATES: *(remains silent.)*

ENVOY: Of course, you could say that our laws reflect the people's wisdom, whereas those other laws reflect a tyrant's madness. But really it is unimportant who wrote the laws —one fool or five hundred fools. The important thing is for everyone to obey them. Isn't that so?

SOCRATES: *(remains silent.)*

ENVOY: But how do you know if the people really accept the laws? Because their faces look satisfied or because there are processions of boys carrying torches? You know that such things easily can be arranged. Because people may obey laws even while they rebel against them secretly. Thus, your defense of the law is really nothing but the defense of authority. And absolute authority, at that. You are a totalitarian.

SOCRATES: Go on.

ENVOY: No sentence has been carried out in Athens for several years. The condemned simply walk out of prison in broad daylight, go to Pireus, board a ship, and later write insolent letters from Crete or Melos. Sometimes they enclose a few coins "to compensate for the unforgettable time they had in that quaint little hotel at the foot of the Acropolis." We know what hurts you most. Not the Athenian shoemakers' and butchers' lack of philosophical education, but the liberalism of Hellas. Young people have been heard to repeat your aphorism: "Nothing strengthens body and soul so much as early rising and alternative."

SOCRATES: Have you anything else to say?

ENVOY: Yes, I have come to certain conclusions. You have
failed to cure us with logic so now you are trying to save us
with crime. You want us to feel the taste of your blood. You
want new power, even if this means tyranny. For only after
this will we attain a new freedom, a Pericles, symmetry,
beautiful architecture and poetry. And a dignity of life
now possible only in the theater. Basically, Socrates, you
are a politician with a tendency toward coup d'etat. Well,
why don't you say something?

SOCRATES: I am thinking of something—sadly.

ENVOY: Of what?

SOCRATES: I am thinking that there isn't much time left and
that I've set loose a monster.

ENVOY: Try to tame it.

SOCRATES: It's too late.

ENVOY: It's never too late. You're still alive. I'll return tomorrow and I hope to find this cell empty.

Scene 3

GUARD: I didn't care for him too much, this new acquaintance
of yours. A disciple?

SOCRATES: No. A clerk.

GUARD: Penniless also, eh? It's about time you received some
rich people, Socrates. Don't you know a rich banker?

SOCRATES: No.

GUARD: That's a pity. Because, you see, the release tax is quite
low during the first days of imprisonment. Later, the cost of
upkeep is added. I'm not talking about myself, mind you—
my price is always the same: five obols. Whatever the crime.
It's all the same to me whether it's "disorderly conduct
while under the influence of drink" or "matricide." But
first you have to settle matters with the authorities. They
say we must observe the rules of progression in such matters

and I see their point. Otherwise we'd fall into complete anarchy.

SOCRATES: There's that hierarchy of values everywhere, eh?

GUARD: It seems so, doesn't it? Though I must say I'm sorry for you.

SOCRATES: Why?

GUARD: Because you have no friends. So many people come here, but not one of them is willing to help you.

SOCRATES: Some of them would help me perhaps, but I'm too much of a risk. I'm too old, you see.

GUARD: Hey, don't talk that way. If someone were close to you, he wouldn't mind parting with his money. Otherwise —you'll die. Don't you have anything you could sell?

SOCRATES: Nothing.

GUARD: Well, that's that. I saw your wife and sons—they looked shabby. You don't look much better yourself. If only they'd given you a better-looking coat for the day after tomorrow. I would lend you mine, but I'm afraid you'll run away with it to the other side. (*He laughs.*) You know, I even like you. But lots of people don't. They say you're conceited and don't believe in the gods.

SOCRATES: Who says that?

GUARD: People.

SOCRATES: And what do you say?

GUARD: I don't know you well enough. But I think people ought to be respected even when they do believe in the gods. Religion is a beautiful thing, you know. It's easier to love a wife who sleeps next to you—much easier than it is to love Aphrodite. . . .

SOCRATES: What about you? Do you believe in the gods?

GUARD: I believe in them when it thunders. But I pray even when the weather is good.

SOCRATES: To whom?

GUARD: To heaven. When you lift your heart to heaven your whole breast immediately feels warm. (*Plato appears on the staircase.*)

PLATO: We are here, Teacher. Shall I call them in?

SOCRATES: Come in. (*To the Guard.*) They've interrupted us. You can't imagine how bored I get during these lectures. It's different with you. With you, a person gets down to basic issues right away.

GUARD: Listen, Socrates, speak to them. Maybe one of them will put up the money. They say Plato has lots of money.

SOCRATES: All right, all right. Now go away.

Scene 4

(The Disciples enter.)

DISCIPLES: Greetings, Teacher.

SOCRATES: Good day to you. Will Xenophon tell us what we talked about last time?

XENOPHON: We discussed the validity of the equation: reason=goodness=happiness. We defined these terms and mentioned a number of examples from life. Then we discussed the whole thing.

SOCRATES: Who took part in the discussion?

XANTHIAS: I did.

SOCRATES: We are listening, Xanthias.

XANTHIAS: In our city of Thebes, there lived a very wise man called Sophron. When his daughter died—Sophron hanged himself.

PHAEDRAS: That's what happened. And no one said: "Sophron went mad before he died." All anyone said was that he had lost his only daughter.

PLATO: I ask you, Socrates, why Oedipus, who was unquestionably a wise and good man, was not happy? Wisdom is one of the prerequisites of happiness, but there is also fate.

PHAEDO: When I wake up at night and realize that I am, I feel pain. Then I repeat your catechism: Who are you? A man. What is man? An animal that laughs and reasons. What does man need? To know. And what about happiness? Happiness is the child of knowledge. And at such times, instead of fear, I feel a vacuum. I touch my face. And fear returns.

SOCRATES: I thought you were mature enough to understand abstraction. I was mistaken: what you understand is an image. Oh well, since there isn't time to teach you wisdom, let us say something about hygiene. Laches, you're a frustrated poet, aren't you?

LACHES: No, Socrates, I studied sculpture.

SOCRATES: So you have the qualifications necessary to become a philosopher. Imagine that you are making a stone head of Apollo. What would you need?

LACHES: Tools and a block of stone.

SOCRATES: Can you imagine that block of stone?

LACHES: I imagined it before you asked me.

SOCRATES: See, we understand each other perfectly. Say you have a cube. Let's assume that it's a cube with smooth sides; the relationship between its length and its width satisfies us deeply. Then you take your hammer . . .

LACHES: Before I strike, I think that the stone will no longer exist and that I don't know which will be more perfect—the original cube of such excellent proportions or that which the cube becomes.

SOCRATES: Yes. But now you know that in this world all things are created from simple forms and eventually will return to them. Consider calmly the lines that enclose objects: pyramids, spheres, cubes. They are colorless. It seems as if they were placed in space by a hand seeking order. Of all our senses, the eyes are the wisest. Eyes protect the soul from chaos. You are cured by the calmness that descends upon you when you see the contour of a branch against the background of winter sky. You, Phaedo, turn on the lamp when you awake at night. Don't lie in the dark because you'll drown in dark music. Turn on the lamp and look at the objects in your room: it doesn't matter what—a sandal or the edge of a table. Learn something about the world's

surface before you begin looking for its heart. That's
enough for today. Please go.

      (The Disciples leave. Twilight falls.)

Scene 5

SOCRATES *(to the approaching shadows):*
When after the final question
silence falls
and the white stone of peace
begins to break in my fingers
I hear
through the quiet, soft as animal fur
I see
through the dark and white lines
of trembling air
two flutes
two horns
emerging from the brink
of reality.

You come Dionysus
killed one hundred times
and as many times risen from the dead
you who trembled like a fish
in the net of syllogisms
and were dealt a mortal wound
by my mechanical
monster of dialectics
you whom I dragged by the hair
through the streets of Athens
you come and say:
"I and my centaurs
shall recite over your corpse, honorable Socrates,
a solid litany
of laughter."

And further:
"You, poor creature, have labored
to free man from anxiety
and the torture of reincarnation
and that is why you grasped the two most
distant words to sow your comical formula:
reason equals happiness.
Do you hear the roaring laughter?
Do you see the firm belly of
Mother Nature
shaking with laughter?"

To this I answer:
It is indeed not pleasing
to offend the gods and fight the devil
only to have the devil finally defeat you
for in all probability
victory belongs to you
Dionysus.
It is possible—as you say
that reason is the death instinct
echo of nothingness.

You have chased me to this cave
and surrounded me with a crowd
bearing my name
the last temptation,
oh tempter.
They come and ask
who is the real Socrates?
You want my head to reel
from seeing these resemblances
so that I, to ward off madness,
shall kneel before divine carelessness
and the holy play of appearances.
You have two nights Dionysus

to tempt me
and I, two days
to learn patience,
so that at the end
tearing off one mask after another
I read with my dying fingers
my own face.

(*Curtain falls.*)

First Interlude of the Chorus

(*The stage is as it was in the Prologue. Three members of the Chorus sit on the ground, playing dice. The three remaining members stand above them, talking.*)

FIRST MEMBER: What's new in the city?

SECOND MEMBER: Nothing.

THIRD MEMBER: The price of onions went up.

(*Silence, except for the clicking of dice.*)

FIRST MEMBER: They say that the war will start soon.

SECOND MEMBER: Who says so?

FIRST MEMBER: The bankers.

THIRD MEMBER: Oh, they always say that.

FIRST MEMBER: The Spartans are holding one maneuver after another along the border. The war will start in the fall.

THIRD MEMBER: It will or it won't.

(*Silence. The sound of dice on the floor.*)

FIRST MEMBER: It's quiet in the harbor.

SECOND MEMBER: The Phoenicians were supposed to come for ceramics and textiles.

THIRD MEMBER: But they didn't come. One thing is sure, at least. The ship from Delos will arrive the day after tomorrow.

FIRST MEMBER: By the way, what's new with Socrates?

SECOND MEMBER: He's still in jail. Everybody is advising him to escape. But he's stubborn. The demon tells him not to.

THIRD MEMBER: What an eccentric.
>(Silence. The sound of dice is heard.)
FIRST MEMBER: I'll tell you why he doesn't escape.
THIRD MEMBER: Yeah?
FIRST MEMBER: He can't stand ocean voyages. He vomits at the very sight of the sea.
SECOND MEMBER: That's one more proof that he isn't a Greek. He doesn't like the sea and he doesn't like boys. He doesn't like wine, either.
THIRD MEMBER: If you ask me, he's a changeling. They say his great-grandfather on his mother's side was a Thracian slave.
FIRST MEMBER: It's quite possible.
>(Silence. The sound of dice. One of the players gathers up the money.)
FIRST MEMBER: Who won?
FOURTH MEMBER: I did.
FIRST MEMBER: Are you going to continue playing?
FOURTH MEMBER: We'll play until the end. And then again.

ACT II

Scene 1

>(The following day. The stage is the same.)

ENVOY: Is he asleep?
GUARD: Yes, he's still asleep. During the night he cried out in his sleep.
ENVOY: He cried out? What did he say?
GUARD: I don't know. He called to someone and then told him to go away.
ENVOY: Did you get the name?
GUARD: No.
ENVOY: Tell me, do you treat him well here?
GUARD: Sure we do. What do you think? He cried sort of because of himself.

ENVOY: What about his food?

GUARD: Not so good. He says he's hungry. Sometimes he even drinks the oil from the lamp.

ENVOY: Wake him up.

GUARD: Socrates, the gentleman from the Council is here. Get up. You've slept long enough.

(Socrates wakes up, lowers his legs over the side of the bunk and rubs his face.)

ENVOY: Good day to you, Socrates.

SOCRATES: Good day. Don't you see that one can't make drama out of such monotony?

ENVOY: I'm here for the last time.

SOCRATES: Then let's begin.

ENVOY: Here I am. I stood over you while you were sleeping. Your face was a confession. Your sunken temples, drooping mouth and the wrinkles running down your cheeks all say the same thing: you are at the end of your tether. You sleep a lot but you don't get much rest. You wake up disgusted and confused. You feel as if your body were running away from you. Your arms and legs get numb and your heart can't keep pace with your lungs. Only the name unites the loose parts. You are looking forward to the moment when strange hands will dip the name in stone. You are dead tired, Socrates, and dream of a rest that is deeper than sleep.

SOCRATES: (remains silent.)

ENVOY: All this is quite natural. What is not natural is your tendency to become theatrical. We know very well how meticulously you used to prepare your "accidental" meetings with your disciples in the street, forest and market. Foreigners enjoyed this but we always looked upon the whole thing as a farce. Now, faced with death, you are reaching for the mask of tragedy. Socrates who caught cold while returning home from a party and died of pneumonia, or Socrates perishing in jail, condemned by the people who could not bear the burden of his wisdom: the choice is quite easy, isn't it? You've chosen the easier one. Right?

SOCRATES: *(remains silent.)*

ENVOY: And then, what about that school of yours? In a year or two, it will die a natural death anyway, won't it? The young boys who came to you from distant places do not want to study logic forever, do they? They want to know how many gods there are, what supports the earth and what happens to man after death. Of these three questions, you will be able to answer only one, and that only tomorrow. You are escaping into death because of loneliness and isolation. So much for that heroism of yours. Do you know what a defeated leader does?

SOCRATES: I know.

ENVOY: What about it then? They have arranged everything up there. Choose any way you like. If you want, we'll send you a doctor to open the veins painlessly.

SOCRATES: Thank you. I sense anguish in everything you say.

ENVOY: I am tormented by the way you have managed to get yourself tangled up with death. We really didn't want to condemn you. Now, of course, we can't withdraw, and so we appeal to your loyalty. You must disappear before tomorrow. If it's too difficult to escape with your body—leave it here.

(He leaves.)

Scene 2

GUARD: So?

SOCRATES: Nothing.

GUARD: You're in trouble, you know.

SOCRATES: You think so?

GUARD: They've prepared everything up there. They say you could do it today if you wanted. Everything has been arranged.

SOCRATES: My dear man, do you realize that it is necessary to prepare Socrates also?

GUARD: Oh, I can see that it's all the same to you—you're tough. They asked me to try to convince you. Tomorrow there will be a crowd—the women will come and there will be a great clamor. Today you can do it quietly, without any fuss.

SOCRATES: Yesterday you advised me to escape and today you are advising the same thing.

GUARD: No, I'm not. Now everything is prepared.

SOCRATES: I don't think so. What about my disciples? I caught my coat on a bush and I'm afraid to move—I'd be sorry to leave it behind.

GUARD: I can see that you're fishing for that coat. All right, all right. If they don't bring you one from home tomorrow, I'll lend you mine. You can't drink poison in a rag like this.

(He leaves.)

Scene 3

(Plato appears on top of the stairs.)

PLATO: Greetings, Teacher.

SOCRATES: How are you?

PLATO: We've just come from the chorus rehearsal. At your funeral we are going to sing a fragment from Eurypides: "O Fathers' noble offspring, O Mothers' noble offspring." Tomorrow it will be as we arranged, right?

SOCRATES: Yes.

PLATO: We'll come before sunset.
When the last rays
fall upon the sage's brow
his disciples
with coats drawn over their heads
will descend
step by step
into the night . . .

SOCRATES: Did you write an elegy?

PLATO: I don't think you quite understand. I have to give a name to everything I touch.

SOCRATES: Learn geometry, Plato.

PLATO: It may come to that. I'm not happy with words.

SOCRATES: I know.

PLATO: I see the world as if through a broken mirror—cracked and ragged along the edges. There is no connection between the subject and its appearance or between name and thought. I would like to perceive the most minute object accurately, from all angles, from the center, to know what it feels and what it is in the eyes of the stars. If I could perceive that about even the smallest stone, I would be able to establish knowledge about the affairs of gods and men.

SOCRATES: You are suffering from appearances.

PLATO: Yes, the world consists of appearances. Everywhere shadows, nothing but shadows. But what casts the shadows?

SOCRATES: I discussed that with you, Plato.

PLATO: You have always talked about man and what he ought to be, about courage and goodness. These are not the most important things. The world is the most important thing. The secrets of air, light and water. One must also regard man as a thing. This helps one to bear love and death more easily.

SOCRATES: How strange: two demons—poetry and reality—are fighting for you.

PLATO: Let me tell you something else. Yesterday my friend died. At the news of his death, I became inspired. I wrote a poem. And only after I had written it did I begin to grieve genuinely. I began to suffer.

SOCRATES: Write, Plato, write poems. It is necessary to strengthen the world with false tears.

PLATO: Is this all you are going to leave me?

SOCRATES: Yes, that's all.

PLATO: A few sarcastic words.

SOCRATES: A little more than that, Plato. A bit of irony.

Scene 4

(The Disciples enter.)

DISCIPLES: Greetings, Teacher.

SOCRATES: Good day. What did we talk about at the last lecture?

FIRST DISCIPLE: The usual thing: reason equals happiness. We also discussed the various ways of seeing—how one ought to observe the sharp edges of things.

SOCRATES: You must forgive me, but today's lecture will be somewhat chaotic. I'm still under the influence of my dream. I dreamed that I fell asleep at the bottom of a rocky valley. It was night. And quiet. Suddenly, I heard the clatter of hooves. The sound grew louder. I was nearly trampled on. Then, just as suddenly, the sound seemed to go in another direction and it grew quiet again. Very quiet. And then, once more, I heard that terrible, mounting clatter of hooves.

SECOND DISCIPLE: It was Dionysus, Socrates.

THIRD DISCIPLE: He likes to come at night.

FOURTH DISCIPLE: He cast a spell on three girls from our village. They went into the mountains and are now living with wild goats.

SOCRATES: There is no Dionysus. Two hundred years ago, they caught him in the rocky wilderness and flayed him. You are paying tribute to a rotting god. What I am talking about is blood. In us, there is clear blood and dark blood. The clear blood cleanses the flesh and strengthens us. It determines man's shape and accumulates in his skull. The dark blood beats deep within his breast and is the source of the turbid images of soothsayers and poets. The clatter of hooves is the voice of dark blood. Once it reaches the heart, it is impossible to escape from fear.

FIRST DISCIPLE: It seems to me, Socrates, that this dark well exists not only in us, but in the center of all things: in the

93

trembling night air, at the bottom of clear waters, and even within the sun's fist. For you, the world has been cut from stone. But don't forget that the stone's heart sometimes trembles like the heart of a small animal.

SECOND DISCIPLE: Fear becomes linked with fear, and everything that lives and passes gathers courage from fear. We, particles of humid air, flowers and men, unite against inevitable catastrophe.

SOCRATES: Even if it is as you say, we must cut our way up through the chaos of wells to the starlike thing shining above them.

SECOND DISCIPLE: But can we betray the earth?

SOCRATES: There is no you—no tree shadows or birds, no earth, no sky. There is only motionless unity.

SECOND DISCIPLE: Only the integer?

SOCRATES: Without beginning or end, motionless and indivisible.

SECOND DISCIPLE: The body and soul descend into the depths. New creatures wither and are born within the earth's dark interior. Thousands of new creatures, unlike anything that has been before or will be after.

SOCRATES: I see. I do not think I shall convince you. You are too young. You have been deafened by the quarrel between life and death. But some day you will leave this noisy house and begin your journey upwards. The journey towards the motionless, white, indivisible integer. It's late. Go home.

Scene 5

SOCRATES (alone):

I. First, I beg you: do not leave me. Let me feel to the end your cool hand on my brow and your motionless eyes in mine. And the light.

II. Give me a little more strength. You know how I love form and definitive expression. I was always tied to my body and sure of it alone. So when they begin to take everything from me—control of my legs to power of final thought—help me not to cry out.

III. I do not know whether you will want to save anything. They say that you take from scattered bones a small flame that wanders over the world's wet meadows. I do not want such immortality. If I am to exist in any shape, let me be a creature who loves definition.

IV. I thank you for my life, which has been such that I never repudiated reason. Nor was I ashamed of the vertigo that comes from complete consciousness.

V. I never invoked your name. I made no sacrifices to you. I did not encourage my disciples to worship your cult, if only because I knew that to you it was all the same. I worshipped you in conjunction and disjunction, and also in the small temple of syllogisms.

VI. Now, in the final hour, I beg you: do not leave me. Let me feel to the end your cool hand on my brow. And your motionless eyes in mine. And the light.

(Goes to the window.)

Socrates greets the tree outside. We know now that all which must happen, happens. You said that man must not seek his fate. He must mature, grow, throw seeds and shadows—and wait, accepting whatever comes: the spring wind or the ax. My head is full of gray hairs and order. Your head is full of green rush. And yet it is from you that I have learned the wisdom of patience. Socrates pays tribute to your roots.

(Curtain falls.)

Second Interlude of the Chorus

(The stage is set as before.)

FIRST MEMBER: What's new?
SECOND MEMBER: Nothing.

THIRD MEMBER: They say it will start soon.

FIRST MEMBER: What will?

THIRD MEMBER: They don't say.

SECOND MEMBER: What nonsense.

(Silence. The clatter of dice.)

FIRST MEMBER: In the city I heard that a revolution is brewing in Sparta.

SECOND MEMBER: If there's some bloodletting, there may not be a war.

THIRD MEMBER: There always will be wars.

FIRST MEMBER: Until the time when the people take power into their own hands.

THIRD MEMBER: Then the killing of the people's enemies will start. Royalists will cut to pieces the believers in democracy.

SECOND MEMBER: Yes, yes. It's always the same. The same bunch of shrewd ones at the top and cheated ones at the bottom. The same speeches, monuments, prisons.

THIRD MEMBER: The same old game.

(Silence. The clatter of dice.)

FIRST MEMBER: By the way, what's new with Socrates?

SECOND MEMBER: Still stuck in jail. Tomorrow they'll execute him.

THIRD MEMBER: It's quite a mystery, isn't it?

SECOND MEMBER: You know, I believe the whole thing is some kind of political plot. He got money from someone to compromise our system of justice.

FIRST MEMBER: I think it's much simpler than that. Socrates is quite a troublesome character in Athens and nobody really knows what he's like. They want to smash him to bits and see what's inside.

(Silence, except for the clatter of dice. One of the players picks up the money.)

FIRST MEMBER: Who won?

FOURTH MEMBER: I did.

FIRST MEMBER: Are you going to continue playing?

FOURTH MEMBER: We'll play until the end. And then again.

ACT III

Scene 1

GUARD: How are you today, Socrates?

SOCRATES: How are you?

GUARD: I'm all right, but you, poor man, will never see the stars any more. I wouldn't like to be in your shoes.

SOCRATES: It's not bad, really, except that these last hours are so long.

GUARD: You see, you should have done what I told you yesterday.

SOCRATES: Tell me, have you ever seen any executions?

GUARD: Yeah, a few.

SOCRATES: Do you know what it feels like?

GUARD: When you first drink the hemlock, you feel needles all over your body. Then you become numb, as if you had drunk heavy wine. Your head functions the longest. You can still speak. Then there's hiccoughs and shivering. And that's it. You know yourself what comes after that.

SOCRATES: Do I?

GUARD: To make the poison work faster you should move about.

SOCRATES: Ah, there you are. That's good advice. You are a real friend.

GUARD: Young people react faster than old ones. It all depends on your circulation. You should move around a lot. You have permission to take a longer walk than usual today.

SOCRATES: Fine.

GUARD: Let's go then.

Scene 2

(Xanthippe enters and sits down on the bunk. A few minutes later Plato enters.)

PLATO: How are you?

XANTHIPPE: How are you?

PLATO: Waiting for him?

XANTHIPPE: Yes, I am. I thought it all would be over by now.

PLATO: We are waiting for the ship to come.

XANTHIPPE: Will it come today for sure?

PLATO: Definitely. It should be in by now.

XANTHIPPE: It should, shouldn't it? I am very uneasy about all this. Yesterday he laid his head on my breast and began to shake.

PLATO: Are you afraid for him?

XANTHIPPE: No, I am afraid for myself. I'm old, you see. There isn't much room left in me for emotion. I want him to leave me just as he was always—unknown.

PLATO: Frankly, I've always wondered what the two of you had in common.

XANTHIPPE: I met him on the street one day, and then he began to follow me like a shadow. I felt his eyes on my hair, my face, my skin. Argus.

PLATO: People would call it love at first sight.

XANTHIPPE: It was fear. At that time, Socrates was a tough young man. He was liked—which means he was average. The eyes that looked at him were friendly, expecting nothing.

PLATO: Do you mean to say he saw a question in your eyes?

XANTHIPPE: No, fear. He frightened me, as would an animal. And I think that because of this Socrates came to the conclusion that there was an unknown force within him. So he began to look for it.

PLATO: His wisdom was his strength.

XANTHIPPE: You are mistaken, Plato. His strength was his mysteriousness. He saw it in my eyes. Man is blind about himself. He must have mirrors or the use of other eyes. He loves—thus he stares at himself.

PLATO: And so you discovered his secret?

XANTHIPPE: No, Plato, one doesn't discover secrets. Indeed,

that was where Socrates made his mistake—for it was he who tried to untie them as you untie sandals. Anyway, the most important thing was for me to become free of fear. I thought that the best way would be for me to marry him.

PLATO: Forgive me for saying so, but this doesn't sound very logical.

XANTHIPPE: Yes, it was a mistake. I still remember the first night. He was heavy as stone and silent. He wanted to hear the first word from me. If I had said to him then: "Socrates, you will be a king," he would have become a king.

PLATO: You said that he would become a philosopher.

XANTHIPPE: No, I said nothing. I was ashamed, so I shut my eyes and clenched my fists. He ought to have asked as all men do: "Darling, are you happy?" I would have lied to him and from then on I would have been happy. It's even possible I would have loved him.

PLATO: I see. Hatred appeared instead?

XANTHIPPE: Evidently, simple things are easy to figure out. Yes, hate appeared. It walked behind him like a huge shadow. And again he thought he was great. For the second time his greatness was enclosed in me, in my hate.

PLATO: One might believe there was no Socrates outside you.

XANTHIPPE: He was, however. As soon as he saw that he could not get anything out of me, he stopped noticing me. He even avoided calling me by name and was afraid to use the indicative pronoun. He would say: "A mother should concern herself with her children's education," or "Disorder in the kitchen signifies disorder in the soul." Unable to talk straight, he began to think in abstractions.

PLATO: Really, this is a bit thick. I think you're exaggerating your role, Xanthippe. To the public—if I may use the term —Socrates is the creation of his disciples. When they discovered him some years ago, he was like a street singer— talented but uneducated. He didn't know Homer, his dialectics were those of an amateur and he had no metaphysical interests. To put it briefly, he was a primitive. A whole system of extra training had to be arranged for him. He was made to converse with so-called incidental men—from shoemakers to sophists. It was a tremendous job.

XANTHIPPE: We are arguing about the real Socrates as if we were rolling dice for his coat. I think we can agree on a temporary definition: the real Socrates is the one who must die.

PLATO: Yes, he has to die regardless of his philosophical school. He was a star in Athens' intellectual firmament and he must die before they begin analyzing the nature of his brightness. Before they ask him about his system. Only we know that there is no system. To keep this secret, Socrates must be sacrificed. The rest belongs to the commentators.

XANTHIPPE: Socrates must die so that Xanthippe does not fall in love with him. When he put his head on my breast a few days ago, I felt a strange warmth. He was small and helpless. What do you think—is he afraid of death?

PLATO: How could he be? At any rate, not since he solved the problem of the soul's immortality.

XANTHIPPE: I'm not asking you what he thinks of the soul but whether he is afraid of death.

PLATO: Ask him yourself.

XANTHIPPE: I assume he'll be sincere.

PLATO: Sincerity is the final mask worn by a living man. Death puts on the next one.

XANTHIPPE: Which one is that?

PLATO: Peace.

Scene 3

(Socrates enters.)

SOCRATES: Greetings. Did you come to say goodbye?
XANTHIPPE: Yes.
SOCRATES: Goodbye then, Xanthippe.

XANTHIPPE: Goodbye, Socrates. I do not reproach you for anything.

SOCRATES: Thanks.

XANTHIPPE: Now all that we disagreed about is unimportant. Is there anything you need?

SOCRATES: I need quite a few things, Xanthippe. But I must try to get them by myself.

XANTHIPPE: What shall I say to our sons?

SOCRATES: Tell them that their father thought about them on his last day and prayed to the gods that they would grow into fine citizens. What do you think, Plato, will they blame me for dying in prison?

PLATO: I'm sure they won't.

SOCRATES: I think so, too. There is no subject on which the Athenians are unanimous. Farewell then, Xanthippe, and thanks for everything.

(Xanthippe leaves.)

SOCRATES: And what about you, Plato? What shall I wish for you?

PLATO: I have a final favor to ask, Socrates.

SOCRATES: What is it?

PLATO: Can we be present at your death?

SOCRATES: Is it necessary?

PLATO: You promised.

SOCRATES: Yes, but I still have to settle many things with myself.

PLATO: We won't disturb you now. We'll come just before the execution. You'll be a hero dying with a chorus in the background.

SOCRATES: All right, all right. But I would have preferred someone else to supply the chorus.

PLATO: And will you tell us something about the soul's immortality? It would be a most appropriate ending.

SOCRATES: Please go now, Plato. Don't come until just before the execution.

(He withdraws to the corner. The stage lights cast the

shadow of a spider's web; he seems entangled like a fly.)

SOCRATES: Today, I called you for a long time, but you must have been busy. Probably you've been watching. I must admit I like you best in this role: two busy coral eyes and perfect control over your sympathies. People say this is also part of cruelty. I don't know. I only know that keen observation is one half of philosophy. The other half is a strong net. It is important that the net not be noticeable at first. The victim feels he is caught by the air. He believes he is fighting against one of the elements and in this way explains his defeat. Only afterwards does he see the thin threads binding his body. Then, by means of reason based on rational premises, you can begin to prove to him that he will die. I did it differently. I assumed that my victims were rational animals and so I began with the definition of syllogisms; it was only later that I showed them—very discreetly—the perspectives of metaphysics. You turned out to have been the better philosopher; first render your victim helpless, throw him into the bottomless pit and then add fear, suffering and so forth. I cannot help but admit that your method is better. And because the results never can be checked—your philosophy is superior. However, you had an easier task. Your victims were weaker than you, whereas there was a difference in kind between myself and the specimens I hunted. My net had to be strong and to inspire confidence. When finally, I got caught in it myself, I could not show them that I was able to break the net as if it were a spider's web and cross to freedom on the other side. It is a question, you understand, of the respect one has for one's net. A moral question.

Scene 4

(*Crito is shown in by the Guard.*)

CRITO: You wanted to see me, Socrates?

SOCRATES: Ah, there you are, Crito. Please sit down. I need you badly.

CRITO: I suppose you want to write your last will.

SOCRATES: Heavens no, nothing of the kind. Here I occupy myself only with foolish things. You don't by any chance remember the name of our mutual friend? The little red-haired boy? He used to live next door to us at the corner of Sandalmakers Street. We spent a lot of time together.

CRITO: Do you mean Menaichmos? The one who afterwards went to Melos with his parents? He had a harelip.

SOCRATES: Yes, that's the one.

CRITO: Menaichmos . . . the red-haired boy . . . harelip. Very strong. He could beat us all in a fist fight. But you were a better wrestler. As soon as you put a lock on someone— that was the end of him.

(They both laugh.)

SOCRATES: And do you remember our boat races?

CRITO: Of course. The best boats were made of bark. They never sank. To make them go faster we attached a piece of iron underneath. The season would start about the middle of April at the northern brook, right? The finish line was near the bridge. The winner would take his opponent's boats. You once beat Menaichmos and he couldn't forgive you. He hid and threw a stone at you. It cut your forehead. We thought he had killed you.

SOCRATES: I remember. When I got home that day, my face was covered with blood. All the same, my mother gave me a good beating. Yes, Crito, every victory bears the seed of defeat.

(They both laugh.)

CRITO: Yes, yes, Socrates. They couldn't manage you at all at school. Finally, whenever something happened and they couldn't discover who did it, everyone would say: It must have been that devil Socrates.

SOCRATES: The time with the beetles, do you remember that?

103

CRITO: And the time you set fire to the corridor? The whole school nearly burned to the ground. Antiphonos screamed as if he were being flayed alive.

SOCRATES: Antiphonos was the grammarian, wasn't he?

CRITO: No, he was the geometrician. Very dull. Do you remember how he used to say: "Listen, fools, what is the tangent alpha equal to? The tangent alpha equals . . ."

SOCRATES: Was he the one who couldn't stand it when he found grass snakes in his pocket?

CRITO: Yes, he's the one. You know, sometimes I dream about exams. They keep asking me things and I never know the answers. I don't even know what the sum of the corners of a triangle is.

SOCRATES: My, my, the good old days.

CRITO: Beautiful, even if our hands and bottoms were red as beetroot from being punished.

SOCRATES: How many of us are left?

CRITO: Two—in Athens. The rest have either emigrated or died.

SOCRATES: Why are you looking at me like that?

CRITO: I'm trying to find . . .

SOCRATES: What?

CRITO: The scar from Menaichmos' stone.

SOCRATES: It healed. That was a long time ago.

CRITO: Come a little closer. I remember it was just above your eyebrow. There, there it is! Small, hardly visible, but it is there. I am sure that's it.

SOCRATES: Thanks for coming, old friend. It helps at such moments to be with someone who remembers your childhood.

CRITO: I will close your eyes. What else can I do?

SOCRATES: Nothing. But we had a nice talk.

CRITO: Though I think reminiscing like this softens a man.

SOCRATES: Not at all. Now I really can say: There was a man called Socrates.

Scene 5

(The Disciples enter.)

PLATO: The ship has arrived.

SOCRATES: That's good news.

FIRST DISCIPLE: We have come to say farewell.

SOCRATES: Farewell, then. Don't blame me for teaching you so little. Teaching is a rather difficult business. You'll know something about it when you become fathers.

(The Disciples wait in silent anticipation.)

SOCRATES: I see that you are waiting for the final lecture. You want to hear something about the immortality of the soul— as Plato demanded. But wouldn't it be better to talk about the weather? About the recent frost and the danger it presents to the vineyards? Although the shepherds say that the warm rains will come soon and that everything will be covered with green. Everybody will be covered with green.

CRITO: Listen, my friends. Don't bother him now. We'll stay here with him until the end, close his eyes, pray for him, and go home when it is over. But let's leave him in peace now.

(Silence for a long time. The tension is unbearable.)

SOCRATES: They are coming.

CRITO: Not yet, it's only your imagination.

SOCRATES: I prefer to speak now. An hour before my death my friend comes to see me. By the way, I said, "before my death." The pronoun is significant, isn't it? What does it signify? It signifies that we try to get used to the matter at hand, to adjust to it. This, it seems, is the only correct way. And the alternative: to regard it as violence and rebel against it. This leads to religion or insanity. A philosopher should adapt to necessity. But now the term death itself seems wrong to me. It's an abstraction, and an improperly constructed one at that. It encloses a long fragment of time called dying. All this—staring eyes, thumping heart, harsh breathing, raising oneself on one's elbow, groaning with the last breath, and finally, the stiff strangeness and stubborn silence of the body. All these states are described by a single term. A brief word, as if cut with a knife.

I want to draw your attention to the continuity and many phases of the phenomenon. Equally significant is our inability to determine the exact point at which the process begins and where it definitely ends. This leads one to the conclusion that life is full of death and death full of life's spasms. Or rather, that we die from the moment we are born and that you, at the peak of your life, are already knee deep in death.

We can express this in geometrical terms as a sector or fragment AB along which moves the point X.

This becomes even more complex when we decide to illustrate it using the image of the circle. Having toured the circumference, point X arrives at the point where it started. This would suggest the possibility of another start and thus lead us to a concept of infinity and immortality. This undoubtedly is more interesting, if only because the first concept—that of disconnected and suddenly interrupted fragments—leads to chaos, even if we assumed the existence of mechanical necessity or any other concept uniting these fragments into a rational view of the world. How should one declare oneself? . . . I think they are coming.

PLATO: Yes, they are coming.

(Two Guards and a Boy with a goblet enter. Socrates drinks from it. He walks up and down the cell and stops. He staggers. The Disciples take hold of his arm and lead him to the bunk.)

GUARD: Your legs are affected already, poor man.

SOCRATES: Yes. (After some time, pronouncing each word separately.) Don't forget to offer a cock to Asclepius.
(Then feverishly and incoherently.)
Yes, Polos . . . justice . . . to offer . . . whole life . . . Apollo . . . Polos . . . remember . . . whole life . . . why . . . is not . . .

(It is quiet.)

PLATO: Before we take off his mask, let's establish his last words: "Do not forget to offer a cock to Asclepius." All that followed was raving. We record these last words so that there will be no arguments.

FIRST DISCIPLE: What do you think his words meant?

SECOND DISCIPLE: They simply refer to some sacrifice that is due, which he suddenly remembered he had forgotten.

THIRD DISCIPLE: Eh, that would be rather commonplace.

FOURTH DISCIPLE: Anyway, he was never ill.

PLATO: I see in them a metaphorical expression, something in the style of a grand metaphor.

THIRD DISCIPLE: A grand metaphor?

PLATO: Yes.

(Curtain falls.)

Epilogue of the Chorus

FIRST MEMBER: What's new?

SECOND MEMBER: The buzzing of mosquitoes.

THIRD MEMBER: The plague already.

FOURTH MEMBER: Small Erinyes.

FIFTH MEMBER: Everything is smaller nowadays.

SIXTH MEMBER: Even the gods with their epidemics.

FIRST MEMBER: And besides that—calm.

SECOND MEMBER: Calm and malaria.

THIRD MEMBER: Malaria signifies the end of civilization, and calm the pangs of conscience.

FOURTH MEMBER: We are more silent about him than about anyone.

FIFTH MEMBER: About whom?

FOURTH MEMBER: Socrates.

FIRST MEMBER: No, the whole thing wasn't right.

SECOND MEMBER: Innocent blood has been shed.

THIRD MEMBER: Amends will have to be made.

FOURTH MEMBER: He was burned at the expense of the state.

107

FIFTH MEMBER: Some people are beginning to hint about building a monument to him.

SIXTH MEMBER: And even about beatifying him.

FIRST MEMBER: Look, here comes the keeper of corpses.

SECOND MEMBER: He always has his wits about him . . .

THIRD MEMBER: And is always in the know.

KEEPER: Greetings, honorable citizens, what are you talking about?

FOURTH MEMBER: Socrates.

KEEPER: Are you speaking of him in a mystical or in a patriotic way?

FIFTH MEMBER: Mainly in the former.

KEEPER: Nonsense, my dear people. It's a simple matter really. Socrates was of proletarian origin. His father tried to make a living from his workshop, but he didn't get on too well. Competition, huge factories, big manufacturers—you understand. Socrates had to go out on the streets and earn his living by talking—so he became a philosopher because of economic conditions.

FOURTH MEMBER: Who made a martyr of him?

KEEPER: He did himself—or to be more exact, it was the result of his inability to understand the mechanism of history. As a proletarian, he ought to have become an exponent of the proletariat's goals. He should have become a people's tribune, an agitator. His platform was prepared for him: to fight, on the one hand, against the reactionary upper bourgeoisie, and on the other, to seek for close contact with the progressive lower bourgeoisie. Simple, eh? But he preferred aristocracy and its precious disputes—about what is good and what is evil, about abstract justice from the moon. So he fell from the moon straight into jail. Thus one pays for betraying one's class. Bye, bye. Fight mosquitoes and idealism.

(Exit Keeper.)

FIRST MEMBER: You know something? Let's play craps.

SECOND MEMBER: A good idea.

108

THIRD MEMBER: Let's play.
FIRST MEMBER: We'll play until the end and then again.

Translated by Paul Mayewski

Notes for a Biography

In a brilliant essay by Adolf Rudnicki I recently read a few sentences on young people who "about the year 1950 came out with their thin books and immediately won prizes . . . using images striking us today as ludicrous, but at that time received with reverence by official critics." The eminent writer-psychologist quotes with full approval the words of Professor N., spoken at the time most critical for him: "They do not break down. . . . They have merely passed from one trade to another; they have changed their profession and they do not even know that it is possible to break down."

I have lost all desire to write about those whom Toeplitz calls "pampered boys." I do not know much about them and, what is worse, I do not possess the key with which Dostoevsky unlocks his unfathomed souls. Instead, I wish to address myself to others: Harasymowicz, Krysko, Drozdowski, and Lej, and tell them quite simply about myself and my generation: about the gloomy sectarians, the dull schematists, the blind eulogists of reality, the muzzlers of the literature of the decade, the epigonists of Mayakovsky, the dry-as-dust doctrinaires—all of them devoid of talent and imagination; about us, too, I shall write, who lived a long time ago, in another epoch, and who, when we died, were buried and consigned to eternal perdition. Our souls wander about in Hell, our names serve as small change to publicists, and our bodies. . . . With amazement I touch this twenty-nine year old body of mine: it *is*, it endures, it breathes, it even thinks and remembers. An enigma of Nature?

Well, listen to how things really were.

A Schematist's Youth

When in March, 1945, I came back to my native land, traveling in a heated boxcar or "teplushka," I arrived in Lodz as an uncouth and plainspoken lad from a small town on the Niemen. My first question upon crossing the threshold of the District Committee in Gdanska Street was: "Is the P.P.R.[1] the Communist Party?" The female comrade behind the desk, startled by my question, began to explain to me something or other about that democratic bloc; suddenly she stopped and asked suspiciously:

"But what makes you so interested in *that?*"

"I want to join the Communist Party."

I was admitted in a way not according to regulations. After a brief quiz ("Who were Marx and Lenin?"), the secretary of the District Committee, who was seeing me for the first time in his life, duly approved my registration. Then, handing me a white membership card, he asked: "Where do you want to go—to the Youth Section, the Security Office, or the Political Education Group?"

I would certainly have preferred to join the Security Office but for the fact that a few days later there came a fourth alternative. *Glos Ludu* published my first rhymed invective, formless and ringing with passion, under the title of "Before

[1] The Polish Workers' Party.

Berlin," whereupon I was assigned to cover local news.

Thus my conscious life began, or rather my responsible life—a life wherein Party, work and poetry were not separate entities but wherein Communism was our supreme poetry and our daily toil, poetry itself being only a way to Communism and a life sacrificed to Communism. You may smile wryly at such old-fashioned grandiloquence. Too bad, but that is how it was.

In the fall I enrolled at the University. Those of us who were members of the Polish Workers' Party and of Zycie (Life) were a mere handful. We had no time for studies, and besides we did not worry too much about them. We were "making politics." We indulged in no idle talk, and every conversation became an ideological contest. This applied even more to seminars and examinations. Some professors were notorious for flunking students who wore the badge of the Union of Fighting Youth. However, in spite of universal ill-will, we asserted our views and we proclaimed the slogans of the Party and the tenets of Marxist ideology (and what if that was perhaps a simplified Marxism-for-Youth?). We aggressively circulated Kuznica (Smithy) and a mimeographed sheet of our own. There were dramatic situations, too. At schools of higher learning there were active clandestine groups and legal organizations, such as "Wici"[2] under the leadership of Mikolajczyk. Several times they succeeded in mobilizing the majority of the students to open provocations and demonstrations. Yet we always stood up to them.

And to whom did we not stand up in those hectic years! To armed gangs and kulak agitation in the villages, to Catholic Sodality fanatics, to the black market operators of Piotrkowska Street, to revisionists of Marxism in the allied Union of Independent Socialist Youth, and even—hardest and most painful—to striking textile workers. Behind us stood the Party and it said: It is necessary. And we knew that victory depended upon us—that victory which at the time was not yet

[2] A youth organization affiliated with the Polish Peasant Party.

being taken for granted. We knew no greater joy than that of taking active part in the struggle for the Cause.

But there were also other joys in our lives—lives exhausting, nerve-wracking, and sometimes even hunger-ridden. I understand that Marxism today, taught as it is by bored commentators, may sound to the ears of the young like so much vapid talk. Bah! Even Mayakovsky, crammed into school texts, would get transmogrified into Asnyk.[3] At that time, however, we had no thirst for Agatha Christie. In those days what excited and intoxicated us like the most thrilling novels were modest pamphlets published by Ksiazka (Book): *The Communist Manifesto, The Development of Socialism from Utopia to Science, The Infantile Disease of Communism.* . . . We knew by heart Mayakovsky's "All Right" in Sandauer's translation, as well as "Granada," "A Word About Jakub Szela," "No Pasaran". . . . Some experts today hold that those poems sounded too blatant for our Revolution. Such a thought would never have occurred to us at that time.

I made friendships then such as I have never made since. What a joy it was to shake hands with new comrades! We had no concern then for questions of morality and monogamy, but it seems to me that there was little prudery and debauchery, and a great deal of sincere human beauty in the relations between the sexes.

How many more such joys one could list! Grzegorz Lasota, who may have been fifteen years old when he joined the Party, reminisced in one of his later articles about our night watches, and "our happiness in owning our first pistol." And there was the happiness of our first independent formulation—whether in a speech or in a poem—of the great common Truth, and the happiness of our first victorious discussion with a better informed opponent.

But for all that we were very one-sided and primitive. We failed to understand many cultural problems and underestimated the activities of those elder, well-educated comrades

[3] Nineteenth century Polish poet.

who were serving the Revolution "merely" with their pens. Often we were unable to grasp the meaning even of great masterpieces of art unless they referred directly to the Revolution. Many a basic book which you younger comrades have studied in high school simply remained unknown to us. Added to the vital and inevitable antagonism toward our reactionary milieu was a quite unnecessary antagonism to cultured, progressive men of letters, which later on caused us a great deal of harm.

In the fall of 1946 someone introduced me to a seminar run by *Kuznica*. There I found a bevy of girls, whom I knew to be students of Polish literature, devoutly absorbing the Marxist Revolution from the lips of a witty and well-known critic. He was liberally sharing with his audience an original analysis of an outstanding work of our nineteenth century literature. I sat gloomy and humiliated. I knew the book from hearsay only! I decided to buy it the following day. On the next day, however, I was delegated by our section to be a member of a Party trio in one of the electoral districts in Lodz. At that point everything else ceased to exist.

Electoral action! That meant away with studies—no more seeing friends and having dinner—not even thoughts of anything unconnected with elections! Even at night we dreamed of victory in the elections. We knew everybody in our districts: allies, enemies, fence-sitters. And everybody knew us. One secret, however, had to be carefully kept from the district activists: that one or the other of the leaders of our trios was not himself a voter. Under the electoral law at the time, no one under twenty-one years of age could vote. Knowledge of the fact that some of us had not yet reached that age might, we feared, jeopardize the Party.

One day, on Piotrowska Street, I met an editor of *Kuznica*. He gave me a friendly smile and asked:

"Why don't you come to our seminar?"

"Elections," I mumbled.

"Yes, of course, we all. . . . But when the elections are

over, please do come. When, do you think? In two weeks?"

I did not reply. Just at that moment I realized that now I would never again go to *Kuznica*.

What else shall I tell you about those days—perhaps the most beautiful time of my life? This will do. But still let me mention some poems of mine dating from that period. I shall not try to explain to Andrzej Jasinski why I sang of printed calico on the shelves of our first State Department Store. Nor shall I try to convince him that for us Swierczewski[4] was not a "faraway model" whose tragic and heroic death was apparently to be reinterpreted "in terms of our current needs." But I shall no longer check my impatience at having to listen to the inopportune defenders of the new poetry, whom we know only too well. We constantly rubbed shoulders with all of them, those otherwise decent people to whom our passions were entirely alien, who did not trust any of our emotions, and who did not accept the tiniest bit of our own experiences and observations. How easy it was for them to anatomize and expose our clumsy poems! They saw that the ne'er-do-well Bratny was imitating Expressionists; Holda, Imagists; and Mandalian, Mayakovsky. They thought they knew everything about us. They also imitated to some extent, but discreetly, without fanfare, without offense to anybody. They did not claim then, as they are wont to do today, that it was *their* chamber poetry that mirrored the Polish Revolution. And it must be only in retrospect that they have evolved their pet theory about the gentle, meditative character of that Revolution. But what they now present as an objective result of their current reflections and comparisons is only a repetition of their former reaction to a certain kind of experience alien to them, and, of course, to a poetry equally alien.

Anna Kamienska genially explains to critics that "as soon as a poet writes that he has not divided people into friends and enemies, it means that he *has* divided them and very definitely so." This praiseworthy knack of reading between the

---

[4] Communist leader in the Spanish Civil War.

lines, however, forsakes her when she reaches for the literature of the early postwar years, with its call: "There is no death! Man does not die!" Following in the footsteps of Przybos, who has already sought several times to heap ridicule on the title of my first volume of poems, and also on that of a novel by Brandys, Kamienska suggests that the problem of death did not even exist for the cocksure and clamorous authors of the period 1945-1948. Or is it true, perhaps, that "as soon as a poet writes that there is no death, there *is*, and who knows how near at that!" And it was no longer death in a concentration camp, an obsession we would reproach Drozdowski for, and how unjustly! This was the death of members of the Polish Workers' Party, the Union of Fighting Youth, the Security Office—and it was we who were the members of the Polish Workers' Party, the Union of Fighting Youth, the Security Office! It was death from around a street corner, on the highway, or on the outskirts of a village. We were eighteen- or twenty-year-olds, we made the Revolution, and that is why we went to the countryside but did not always return. That is why we went to meetings of the consumers' cooperatives, went in general wherever we were sent. Kamienska maintains that we were merely rebelling against "the sophisticated neckties of the bourgeoisie!" Do not believe it, Drozdowski! We had more dangerous and powerful adversaries. And we wanted to live, but never to surrender. And with death often so near us we rebelled against it, and cried out in our poems: "There is no death!" And we were believed by our comrades, not all of whom have remained alive to bear witness to those events.

The Years of Glory

But do not think that I am going to defend everything that has happened since.

In *Zycie Literackie* (Literary Life), there recently appeared a review of my selected poems by Wladyslaw Maciag.

As I read it I grew angry and outraged. How many poems, still dear to me, had been neglected or passed over by the critic! How many had he judged with excessive severity! Oh, pangs of wounded vanity! How much more would you have preferred, though granting shortcomings and failures a hundred times over, to have had justice done to what had been accomplished, if only the praise had balanced the blame! And yet Maciag is right in his main observation, however unpleasant this may be to me. For quite soon after the publication of my first volume of poems there followed, in the words of the reviewer, "a crisis of the artistic attitude," a kind of artistic breakdown. Let me be more precise: this was a crisis of the ideological attitude, an ideological and moral breakdown.

How did it come about? Mandalian is not wrong in pointing to the general distortion in the life of the Party as fundamental to the distortions in literature. But we must go into this matter a bit more in detail. I am not sure that our defeat was inevitable.

It is so difficult to evaluate those years because in them two great contradictory processes were inextricably intertwined. The Revolution triumphed, grew in scope and forged ahead, and at the same time it retreated and succumbed to distortions. We writers were both the subject and the object of those two processes.

By the end of 1947 or thereabouts, there began to shape up in Warsaw a sort of literary group. Drawn to it were veterans of the Union of Fighting Youth, along with some former Home Army men who were making their way painfully into the ranks of the Party, not from light-mindedness or opportunism but from deep conviction and fervor. There came others, too, whose life stories were different, whom "life had not treated with kid gloves" either. Our common characteristic was a considerable (excessive, according to some) sense of belonging to the same generation and sharing a common ideology. We wanted and endeavored to create a revolutionary art. Stubbornly, we strove after ideological and artistic self-determination, seeking to present the reader with the literature we advocated, one of political and Party commitment. The monthly *Nurt* (Current), edited by Tadeusz Borowski, was shut down after two issues had appeared. For a few months, Tadeusz Kubiak and I collaborated on the biweekly *Po Prostu* (Plain Talk), but after a row with its publishers, the general managers of *Zycie* (Life), we again had to say good-bye. The ill-starred Nieborow demonstration of January 1948, when to a man we served notice of our refusal to obey the mentors on the staff of *Kuznica*, resulted in closing the columns of that review to us. I remember a meeting in the home of Hela Jaworska in the course of which we put together the first edition of a supplement to *Glos Ludu* (People's Voice)—the weekly *Do Rzeczy* (Down to Brass Tacks). Soon afterward some mysterious order broke up and scattered the galleys in the printing shop, though they had already passed the censor. The last review to be liquidated through "our fault" was the respectable *Odrodzenie* (Renascence), which had been careless enough to extend its hospitality to Roman Bratny. After the publication of my "Battle for Mayakovsky" and Borowski's "Conversations," such disintegration set in that not only did *Odrodzenie* itself go to pieces, but its monolithic staff as well, shattered beyond repair.

However, none of these blows proved catastrophic. So long as we believed in our cause (it was not without its misunderstandings and damaging judgments), so long as we fought for it, so long as we felt that we were the literary vanguard of the Party—we were not lost. Not until after several conferences in cozy offices, long Party meetings, and official dicta published in the press, did we stop trusting our consciences. Only then did we yield to the pseudo-Party pressures of demagogues and look upon ourselves as contaminated, and upon our judges as simon-pure. Not until we had identified the machine that was crushing our backs with the Party itself, and not until we had gone down on our knees before its higher rationale, did we suffer lasting defeat.

The "Pimpled Boys," who in the years 1950-1952 rallied around *Nowa Kultura* (New Culture) and *Sztandar Mlodych* (Banner of Youth), were no longer revolutionaries. Yes, Mandalian is telling the truth when he says that "we wanted to make out of literature a weapon of the Revolution, our one principle being the partisanship of Art." The fact was that the Revolution we defended had acquired counterrevolutionary features, while our concept of partisanship had already assumed the character of a myth.

For myself, I think I can pinpoint the very moment of my breakdown. When I wrote a letter to *Trybuna Ludu* (People's Tribune) to rectify the views attributed to me, and to demand *honest discussion* for the benefit of both literature and the Party, I was still myself. But when, as a result of their refusal to publish that letter, I convinced myself that what I wanted to say and had said was not important, but that what *was* important was what they said (though perhaps not without malice) they had read "objectively," I ceased to exist as a writer of the Party.

At a subsequent congress (or was it a plenary meeting?) of the League of Polish Writers, held in the summer of 1950, I received rough treatment, to say the least, in a lecture on poetry. In the ensuing discussion I subjected myself to frank self-criticism (in connection with Mayakovsky and "the struggle of generations"). Afterward the lecturer, who happened to be one of the official ideologists of literature, came to me to apologize: "How was I to know that you would subject yourself to self-criticism? Had you forewarned me, the appraisal would have been different."

But I was no longer capable of indignation. It was only a short while since I had been subjected to the laws governing our literary life, but they seemed to me natural and inherent in the Party. Later on I learned to apply them myself, though I never became quite so adept at it as our ideologist, "a Talmudic speculator with a dried-out heart and mathematical bumps on a bald pate," to quote Andrzej Braun.

All this was a consequence of my first surrender.

Today we are amazed when we realize how much harmful nonsense we let ourselves be talked into.

We let ourselves be told that a feeling of loyalty to our generation was improper.

We let ourselves be told that the most dangerous features of our work were "unrestained vagaries," "anti-estheticism," and "primitivism," while the ideal of Socialist poetry should be a well-ordered genteel sentence, the avoidance of over-emotional inversions, and humble submission to the traditional rhythms of the nineteenth century.

We let ourselves be told that reverence for tradition was inherent in prosody itself, and not in love and anger, nobility and independence.

We let ourselves be told that certain names ought not to be mentioned, and that this did not falsify history in any way, but merely gave it revolutionary perspective. But certain other names were to be mentioned constantly, this being not servility but idealism.

We let ourselves be told that our inspiration was a thing to be mustered on command, for occasions such as an anniversary or a jubilee.

We were talked into many things by Dr. Faul and his executive assistant — the erudite one with his mathematical bumps. This was not at all difficult since it was carried out under the auspices of the Party and backed by high revolutionary arguments. And we still wanted with all our hearts to be writers of the Party and of the Revolution. We learned from a poem by Asieyev that even Mayakovsky would have been ready to write in iambs had the Party deemed it necessary. We now allowed ourselves, not without a certain painful satisfaction and pride, to be pressed into what was supposed to be the Party mold; we even lent a hand to our molders, repeating aloud their platitudes and doing our best to help in this transformation of our souls, which were not yet sufficiently social-realistic.

Sometimes other, quite heterogeneous forces allied themselves against us, with a power of obscurantism which in our naiveté we accepted as the voice of the Revolution: now the Humanists of *Kuznica*, whom we repeatedly outraged with a persistence worthy of a better cause; now the "clan of the unshakable ones," the same who today rail at "heroic opportunism" and insist that it was they who popularized the great prototype of the author of "The Bath"; now the "defenders of Polish Culture against the flood of Barbarism," about whom I will say nothing lest I be again suspected of equating, out of malice, politically divergent attitudes. Still, we were ready to fight each of those forces to our last gasp. Only one of them paralyzed us; yet, but for its element of obscurantism, it might well have become our inspiration and our haven. The tragic paradox of such situations is familiar to revolutionaries more experienced than we were at that time.

Did we give our worthy pedagogues no further trouble? I still recall our miniature revolts and attempts at protest. Once, for instance, I took part in editing an anthology of Polish revolutionary songs. In it was a text by an "unknown author" (to all appearances Bruno Jasienski), "March of the Cracow Insurgents," written in 1923. Someone saw fit to alter certain words considered unsuited to the political situation of 1950. For example, the words "Fascist, snooper, and Social-Democratic ruffian" were changed to "Fascist, snooper, and wretched cur." Similarly the second line of:

"For another Poland we shall fight today,
For the Polish Republic of Soviets."
was changed to:
"For our Socialist system."

In a letter to the Department of History of the Party, I objected to this falsification of historic songs, and suggested that we explain in footnotes the circumstances in which the obsolete watchwords had arisen.

My objection went unanswered, and, of course, the "wretched cur" appeared in print, while in accordance with a law now familiar to me, my name was removed from the list of editors of the anthology. This time I was actually grateful for the omission.

I might cite other such miniature revolts and conflicts with editors, publishers and so forth, but these would not alter the fact that our socialist-realistic education was progressing according to schedule in all its general outlines; that we were passing from one class to another without bad marks, in the comforting conviction that we were perfecting our craft and maturing politically. In reality we were getting duller and duller.

Another thing. The completely extraneous activities to which some of us—including the writer—were committed after our surrender also contributed to our decline. Did you read in *Swiat* (World) the story of Piotr Ozanski and Nowa Huta? Well, we became the Ozanskis of literature. We went to peace congresses and youth festivals, sat in presidiums, were elected to executive positions in Z.M.P., Z.L.P., P.O.P., P.K.P.N., T.P.P.R., etc., made speeches, "published opinions on the subject of—," offered literary advice. The further we went along this road, the more formal and sterile did all this busyness become. The less time and zest for writing we had, the more gratification did our overweening conceit derive from the great world of appearances in which we had bogged down. While our vanity and avidity for easy fame and undeserved privileges kept growing, our interest in the life of "ordinary" people—so much poorer, quieter and . . . truer than our own— kept diminishing. We had not yet turned cynics, we did not yet lie consciously, we were still writing for the cause, and not for honors and money—and yet, as well as distorting our consciousness, our twisted lives had already left traces in our work.

I do not damn our creative work indiscriminately—mine or that of others of that period. Whatever was revolutionary in the times found expression in our books. Particularly in fiction — maybe because the writing of fiction was more strongly influenced by the everyday life of the people, by the milieu, by the realities of our personal lives. In my opinion, the actual revolutionary current gave rise to such works of realism as "On the Construction Site," "The Tractors Will Conquer the Spring," "Coal," "Mrs. Dorothy's Troubles," "Lewanty," "In Accordance with the Law." And the poems? Why, we were young, we loved, we suffered, we were most sincerely moved by many things really worthy of our emotions. Most painful to us now is the awareness of what we failed to write about because we did not understand it or see it, or simply refused to see it. The crisis of our poetry arose from being limited to certain phenomena and emotions, excluding others that were less obvious. This is not always possible to detect in a single poem, although it is easy to point out in whole cycles or volumes of poems. "The Spring of the Six-Year Plan" is a characteristic document of such poetry of controlled vision. Its obvious artistic flaws now mean little to me. However, I am still troubled by the memory of the problems and conflicts on which we turned our backs, fallaciously assuming that only a note of fervent affirmation was worthy of the poetry of the Party, mirroring the achievements of socialist progress.

But who were we in reality, with all our pitiable evolution? Did we embody the power of the people, or did we represent the Party itself, as we had a few years before? No, we were merely official troubadours of the Party and of the power of the people. The Party was nothing more than an administrative organ, while the power of the people was a pure abstraction. The entire responsibility for shaping reality had slipped out of our hands. What remained was scrupulous attendance at the "Sections of Creative Arts," and regular payment of membership dues. In our poems, however, we kept swelling with pride: "We, the Party, the working class, the People's Poland!" We did not know what a false and hollow ring those words had acquired.

I would be lying were I to pretend that I felt quite easy about all this. I was not aware of the defeat we had suffered,

I believed with my critics that my new volumes were better than "There Is No Death," but at the same time I felt that I was only chasing my tail, that life was giving me less and less satisfaction, that I was harassed and bored stiff. Suddenly I felt an urge to escape the vicious circle of *Krakowskie Przedmiescie*. In October of 1952 I managed to get away, and went to Moscow to continue my studies.

The Great Despondency

That winter belongs among the harshest of my life. I came to the Soviet Union just at the time the Beria terror was reaching its climax. The atmosphere was charged with mistrust, suspicion, and above all with fear. As a foreigner I soon felt it all the more painfully. Under my very eyes Beria's last great provocation—the doctors' plot—was being staged. I could not, nor did I dare suspect that the whole case was a fabrication for the sole purpose of creating a diversion. But I was frightened by its concomitants: fascization of the whole social atmosphere, savage distortion of human consciousness, demoralization of youth. One day a young Russian poet, whom I considered a model Komsomolec (Young Communist League member), brought me his new poem, entitled "Vigilance" or "Should the Enemy Be Unmasked?" In that poem, written with sincere passion, the affirmation of Communism was shot through with accents that would have qualified it for publication in *Prosto z Mostu*.[5] My efforts to persuade him that there was no place for this in our ideology were futile. He had proofs that there was a place for it, and in general, he knew that there was a place for anything which at a given moment was directly or indirectly supported by him who was the supreme authority in things moral and political. I was helpless. I myself had been affected by the cult of personality, though its more ludicrous features irritated me. I did not yet recognize that cult as the prime cause of all my difficulties in

[5] Prewar Polish publication of rightist tendencies.

breathing freely during my first winter in Moscow. For despite all my efforts I felt like a suspect intruder in a secret fortress rather than a foreign Communist in the first state of workers and peasants.

Naturally I was struck most of all by the distortions in literary life. Bureaucracy, playing-it-safe, administrative pressures, dogma-worship, schematism, and, above all, ruthless authoritarianism—all of these pervaded the state institutions and affected large areas of the literary output. I was already used to the tactical relativism of the critical judgments being applied in Poland, but here the confusion of standards had reached its apogee. How often careerist graphomania was extolled and exalted while at the same time mud was slung at more interesting and ambitious works! One was likewise struck by the discrepancy between personal literary tastes and official pronouncements: thus many a work went unpublished and yet was appreciated in the writers' circles—usually non-political, often downright decadent writing.

All these observations and experiences now threw a sort of retrospective light upon the events in Poland during my previous four years there—from 1948 to 1952. I could hardly help realizing that what oppressed me so painfully here had existed in my country in embryo—not yet developed to its ultimate stage. In my activities, and those of my friends, I saw an adumbration of the same attitudes now haunting me in Moscow. Here, too, I said to myself, the point of departure was the success of the Revolution, and just see what it has led to! All through that winter I waged a lonely struggle against a despair I had never felt before. I kept asking myself: Who am I? What cause do I serve? What is this world I am building and singing about? It never occurred to me to solve my dilemma by going over to the enemy camp, by betraying the ideals of the Revolution; though I did recall individual cases, among them writers who, I realized now, may have been impelled to take the first step on the road to apostasy by experiences like mine. But neither from conviction nor from fear or despair could I ever have chosen the capitalist world. My profound conviction of the justness of Marxism had not been shaken. Its fatal flaw lay somewhere in its practice, but what was it and where? That I did not know. My struggle against bitterness, chaos and despondency had become almost hopeless.

The only thing I was capable of at that time was a decision to oppose the bureaucratization of literature — a decision to take up the cudgels for independence of judgment, full freedom of expression, the right to reveal the whole perceived truth about reality, the right of the artist to breathe freely. If the term current in 1954 had been coined then, I would have formulated my decision in the following words: Upon my return to Poland, I shall join the partisans of "the thaw" in our artistic life. That was a minimal program, but I could not afford to step out of the field of literature and yet remain creative.

Meanwhile in Poland the opposite process, that of the "freezing" of the arts, had advanced still further. From the newspapers I learned of the contemptible machinations in connection with the plays of Berthold Brecht. In one of the reviews I read a denunciation of "ideological contraband" supposed to have been introduced by another review. Private channels brought me the lowdown on other phases of our public life, which in one way or another corresponded to the news from the literary field.

What were the prospects of a positive solution for my problems? Very poor. I have already mentioned one solution that I excluded. But there were other possibilities, such as resigning from life, escaping into drink, etc.; or else attempting to carry out a minimal program, bound to end in defeat and compulsory silence; or, finally, another kind of surrender: suppression of doubt, indifferentism, active participation in the organized falsification of life and literature. Those were not entirely abstract considerations. I would not venture to exclude any of them, because I knew each of these alternatives (and several others essentially similar) from actual experience.

In March 1953 a whole epoch ended. That July—after almost a year's absence—I arrived in Poland. I talked freely of all my observations, experiences, and doubts during the winter just past. I did not conceal them even from the Party officials with whom I chanced to come in contact. But the longest and perhaps most fruitful conversations were those I had with my old friends.

Some turned away from me: "He has broken down, become a cynic, lost his backbone." But with the majority I found a common language.

Through quite different experiences my friends (and not only those of my age) had been brought, by 1953, to a certain intellectual and emotional state which shortsighted observers dubbed a "breakdown." My experiences may have been atypical: after all, the others had not left the country. But that mood of bitterness, doubt and restlessness was typical. Typical not only for writers but for a large number of Party activists. It is misleading to ascribe that mood to a somewhat later phenomenon—the "thaw." I think, on the contrary, that the mood was precisely one of the causes precipitating the "thaw." What made the latter possible in the first place were the events between March and July of 1953, which brought to an end the long years of falsifying the Revolution, of violating the Leninist principles of Party life, and of the cult of personality.

Wilhelm Mach once wrote that he felt outraged at the notion of a "thaw" that had not been initiated by an artist. I personally do not feel humiliated that thanks to the decisive moves of the leadership of the Communist Party of the Soviet Union, and of our own Party, I acquired the vision I had lacked before, so essential for resolving my doubts and unrest. On the other hand, it seems to me of importance that we embarked upon a new era—more propitious to the peoples building socialism, and to socialist art—not as docile agents and barometer-watchers, but as deeply committed participants engaged with all our heart in what was going on, determined to wage uncompromising battle for a thoroughgoing purge of the Revolution, to rid it of all anti-revolutionary and inhuman excrescences.

Not that I would want at this point to create in the reader's mind any impression that the period of my great despondency which began in the fall of 1952 actually ended in 1953 with the liquidation of Beria. No, the more the exposure of errors, degeneracies and plain crimes proceeded—responsibility for which rests not only on their direct inspirers and executors but also on those who feared to oppose them, or who acted out of ignorance or blindness—the more difficult did it become to endure one's soul-searching and breast-beating. A few years earlier I had put part of my heart into a poem about the alleged treason of Yugoslavia. How could I feel otherwise than cheated now that I learned that this, too, had been a provocation? I took time from my soul-searching to give way to relief over the fact that another case had been cleared up, another error rectified. And how could one escape the anguish of realizing the enormity of the crimes committed against the body of the Polish Communist Party? One by one, more cases are gradually being revealed—and though we are more hardened to them than we were a few years ago, each one brings us a new, lasting shock. I do not consider this bad. On the contrary, I feel it to be necessary and unavoidable. There may be even more bitterness and despondency in store for us before we fully revise our views about the course of events in the international revolutionary movement since the death of Lenin. And may this period of despondency last! For it is saner and more fruitful than the era of the great decline, dressed up in super-optimism and bogus revolutionary slogans. It will be hard, but we shall hold out.

And even should our enthusiasm never again be quite so boundless and pure as it used to be in our early youth, even should there always remain in us a grain of skepticism and bitterness—what of it? We shall merely be settling an old account which cannot be evaded.

Starting Anew

Yes—we can well afford it. For all our bitterness and skepticism, for all our countless moral losses, we are still rich. Once again we are becoming Communists—we are becoming the Party.

We were such a Party when we made the Polish Socialist Revolution, when we wrestled independently and responsibly with the reality confronting us.

We ceased to be such a Party when we lost faith in our conscience, when we yielded to the pressure of a pseudo-Party scholasticism, when we accepted as our highest revolutionary virtue the discipline and efficiency of mere Party agents. Nothing depended on us any longer—in fact we ceased to be needed. Our activity had turned into a vain play of appearances.

Today we are needed again and again. Everything depends upon us. We are discovering reality anew, and with our conscience, our indignation and our love we are committing ourselves again to that Revolution. We feel responsible for its methods, its purity, its truth. We are no longer docile —we are alert. We act on our own initiative, out of our need to act. We take up, with all its risk, the great challenge of creating a literature of the Party.

And it is this very thing, not a "confusion among writers," nor a "yielding to the pressure of right-wing elements," which constitutes the meaning of that continuous and still developing "thaw"—if I may still use this poor term.

This concerns not merely my own generation, though we have our part in what is happening.

I have pride and faith in my generation, upon which so much sarcasm and so many expressions of false sympathy are being heaped.

I believe that we will have the courage to do our utmost, intellectually and morally, to further the true revolutionary art of our times.

I believe that we will not lapse into that most dreadful

disease, emotional atrophy, but will move honestly and cordially with our people along the difficult, dramatic and bumpy
road to socialism, always leading and helping them.

I believe that our current editorials, feature articles and
columns will be followed by weightier works, encompassing
the whole of our life, the tragedy and beauty of our revolutionary epoch. We will write novels about real men, our com-
patriots and contemporaries; plays with conflicts essentially
like those of their authors and audiences in real life; poetry
that illumines our age and shines bright in far-off ages to come.

I do not know when we shall find the necessary strength
to create such a literature—tomorrow or ten years from now.
But I do know that we are going in that direction.

I do not think that on the journey before us we shall
have to disown Mayakovsky—the first poet of a stature match-
ing the greatness of our epoch. Once before we heard such
advice and—all the worse for us—we followed it. Today we
hear it again. But this time we will not be so easily swayed.

Besides, we know now that being a bit different does not
make a poetic work alien to the Revolution. In recent years,
for instance, I have learned to appreciate the noble voice of
Mieczyslaw Jastrun.

And I feel in general that the poetry of my generation,
even if it does not follow great masters, will find close kinship
with all art which aims at truth, loves man and seeks his
happiness.

I believe in my generation.

I believe that it will succeed in achieving what it sets out
to do, though it meet with distrust, be hampered in its necessary soul-searching, and either spurred on or shouted down.

Naturally I would prefer to see as few such unnecessary
obstacles as possible.

This is what I wanted to tell you, my colleagues and
comrades, to whom I need not condescend even though you
are somewhat younger than I. I thought that you would find
some knowledge of our ways useful—ways not quite so simple

and unequivocal as they may seem. I know I have not been able to present convincingly all the sundry details of my experience. It is all still too much for me to cope with. But after all, this is not the last time we shall be together.

Many of you genuinely stir my affection, although I do not intend to flaunt it as effusively as do certain older poets, who not so long ago were noted for their emotional restraint and matter-of-factness. I do not quite understand what they are aiming at when they publicly bestow their fatherly kisses on your foreheads. Could it be, as Slucki says, that they are trying to woo new recruits for their dwindling ranks of poetic cadets? I do not think such an undertaking has any chance of success. You come here with your own fresh emotions, with your own vision of the world—and you cannot be squeezed into the strait jacket of the old schools even though they be led by well-eserving pensioners from the former avantgarde.

I will not attempt to analyze your work. What seems most precious in it is a yearning for more purity, the unwillingness to compromise which once spurred us in our own efforts. We did not always live up to it. I want to believe that coming years will be more encouraging to the revolutionary and independent spirit of youth. And I refuse to be counted among those who, hurt by lack of recognition for their past "merits" and "achievements," would seek to tame your youthful ardor.

MOSCOW, FEBRUARY-MARCH 1956.

Translated by Julius Balbin

Pawel Hertz

Recollections from the House of the Dead

Nothing is more difficult than to judge time past. We never can be sure whether it really happened or whether it happened only in our imagination. Caught up in it and wishing to be free of it, do we not eagerly assume that we are already free, judging it only from its appearance? But whatever it is, I believe that the purpose of writing is to put the past on record as a lesson and a warning for today and tomorrow.

Those who despair over "the tragedy of Polish literature" are wrong. Because it was not the tragedy of Polish literature that was enacted on the stage of past years, but the drama of the whole nation. And whoever chooses to advance this tragedy instead of this drama either is lying or has forgotten everything and learned nothing. The most elementary conclusion about the past tells us that no artist can exist apart from the nation. What for many years the cynical teachers of ethics and aesthetics proclaimed in the dumb silence of their lecture halls, each one of us felt as a pressure at every moment. We were taught about things we constantly experienced within ourselves. And this tutoring was very humiliating.

Probably not long from now, the cool, quiet analysis of historical events will show how it could have happened that things despised in the depths of the soul were loudly praised, that there was reasoning about righteousness when there was no right, that fear sealed the lips of the brave and boredom became part of the life of the clever. Literature fell as low as the price of decency, love and daring. Petty scribblers took their place on the platform, conference rooms were converted into nurseries, teachers' pets in clean uniforms recited nursery rhymes, and other children clapped and recited in chorus the names of persons detested by the people. But today, even before the historian issues his verdict, each one of us can and should write his memoirs, his reflections on the past. To know about something and to tell what one knows—these are two different things. A man cries when he is hurt, asks for help when he is threatened, calls to God or human beings when he is surprised in mortal danger. Silence is the sister of death. Let the dead bury the dead; we, the living, must speak aloud in strong voices to banish the phantoms, all the ghouls lurking in corners, all the nightmares and demons invoked by the sorcerer's apprentices.

I shall try to tell it step by step, with good will and according to the best of my knowledge and what I consider to be the truth.

In 1945, I joined a small group of people I had known in times past. Fired with the best intentions, hard-tried by history, richer by experiences we had gained in difficulty—some in conspiracy, others in concentration camps, prisons, Siberian tundras and in a country in flames—we were indeed bound by our common conviction that the writer's duty was to serve his country and his people.

All our practical activity was based on this conviction. Each one of us tried first of all to be himself, to express this common conviction in the most individual manner, to be true to his own nature. We were in accord, but had not yet "agreed."

Documents of these years remain—the periodical published for several years as the fruit of our common effort and, more important, a score of books bearing witness to what each of us felt and thought in this period. I have already mentioned that we were in accord. The basis of this accord was the belief that it was enough to be in harmony on a few basic points concerning general principles of thought and action, and that in no case should there be a desire for identity of outlook. This principle bound our inner and outer lives.

After this brief foreword about myself and the friends with whom I worked for five years on *Kuznica*, a periodical too much praised at the time and later uncritically and categorically condemned, I may now speak in the first person only and try more or less accurately to write my recollections and comments.

The war, and the events which had been my experience since September 1939, had convinced me that literature was an inseparable part of national life and that the artist had to be in tune, above all, with the milieu in which he lived—with the nation. The national disaster of September 1939 was my personal disaster; the loss of the state's independent existence, the ruin of the national organization which was the state, canceled once and for all any illusion that the artist in Poland could be independent and convinced me that only a strong, lasting, independent state could assure art an independent and proper role as an essential part of national culture. I understood that it was therefore in the interest of a strong, independent state to assure art full independence and autonomy, because such an organization can exist only when society expresses itself openly, in full voice and through the arts. To be more precise, I should say that one of the conditions of social development is complete freedom for artists and scientists, and that the condition of cultural and artistic development is the constant, independent national existence of a given society. Since I consider any artistic (or scientific) activity to be humanistic because it is creative, I believe that complete freedom in this sphere contributes to the broadest and most beneficial interests of society. The prejudicial fear of error comes chiefly from the feverish defense of short-lived "truths," and the damage resulting from this defense lasts long after the period in which these "truths" were valued and defended with so much effort and sacrifice has died.

For the artist, or the scientist, there is only one supreme truth, the one which binds him to the community in which he works and lives. This truth is creation, the activity in which thousands of mistakes and blunders are compensated for by one genuine achievement. The same is true of all human activity, art constituting one excellent expression of it, and those who want to shackle this activity by one or another system of limitation and prohibition sooner or later will be defeated. For in art, an unwritten system of restrictions and requirements common to all has existed for ages in the form of a humanistic decalogue, and when the artist ignores this decalogue, he runs the risk of incurring the greatest punishment: oblivion.

So, when I got in touch with this group which accepted as a principle the general postulate of modern humanism and was trying to apply it to the historical conditions in which Polish society found itself after the war, I felt that I should cooperate with them, the more so because among them were people I knew well and was close to. Our individual fates after September 1939 had unravelled in different directions, but this rather guaranteed what to me was essential—the existence of different views on the methods and means of realizing what was foremost at the time and common to all of us—the postulate of a modern, humanistic Polish culture.

During these years, our work, despite all errors in principles and tactics, was able to help shape Polish postwar life, primarily because we were united on a completely volitional basis. We were a literary group based on an historical tradition deeply rooted in us and itself the motor of literary life. The second and equally important factor was the existence of other literary circles and also—a point one shouldn't forget—of other political factions. As for *Kuznica*, the alliance of the periodical, its columnists and the literary group editing it with the political body was of a general nature. Up to 1949, this periodical was a tribune for the free expression of ideas by writers who considered the process of socializing Polish life to be historically correct. As to the means and methods of this process, we differed among ourselves, and these differences are easily seen in the lines of the periodical as well as in our books.

My standpoint was middle-of-the-road, in regard to both a literary and a political program. If, at the time, we had used the terminology of the years to come, it would have been said that I was "leaning to the right." I believed then and I believe now that the process of socializing Polish life will succeed only when it is carried out in such a way that the majority of the nation agrees that the benefits derived from it are worth the inevitable changes it brings. I stood for the conscious reform of Polish life with the participation of the majority of the nation which, after the September debacle, was critical of the prewar period and, after 1945, had been organized under new historical and geopolitical conditions.

I believed that literary life in Poland could develop only in an atmosphere of constant, continuous, discussion, that writers should have full freedom to evaluate the various aspects of Polish life, and that nobody should be disqualified for holding this or that view. Therefore, there was no question in my mind that the only criterion of a writer's integrity should be, as it was before the war, his attitude towards totalitarianism, in all its aspects.

Even in the early years, the democratic rights of those writers who did not hold socialist views were abused. But nevertheless they had at their disposal a public tribune in the form of the press, and they were given the opportunity to speak at rallies without having to fear any kind of punishment;

therefore, polemicizing with them seemed to me proper. In those years, I wrote a column for *Kuznica* in which I evaluated and reviewed the contemporary literary press. In my articles I constantly engaged in disputes with the Catholics—to be exact, with the columnists of the weekly *Tygodnik Powszechny*—and also fought against all attempts to vulgarize artistic problems, pseudo-revolutionary attempts to destroy the natural order of literary problems. I often stood alone among the editors in my views, but despite this I enjoyed a fair amount of freedom.

The first warning, which made me stop my polemics with the Catholics, came in a letter I received at the beginning of 1949 from one of the outstanding columnists on *Tygodnik Powszechny*.

My polemics had been concerned chiefly with literature. I held the view that *Tygodnik Powszechny*, with what to me was false solicitude for literature's conformity with primitively conceived, didactic aims, was promoting the cult of intellectual provincialism. I was opposed to its inherent "schematism," as propagated by the Catholic periodical. I had also complained that this periodical was not involved with literary problems and that all its columns were sacrificed to questions of liturgy and dogma. It seemed to me that a Catholic periodical of *Tygodnik Powszechny*'s level should concern itself with lively, sharp discussions on lively, pressing themes, including those of art and literature. In the letter he sent me, my adversary said that the censor had purposely restricted the possibilities of printing discussions on cultural and literary subjects; the aim of this was to prevent the periodical from taking part in the discussions and to create the impression that Catholic writers and columnists had nothing substantial to say on cultural problems and were interested exclusively in religious problems that were of no particular interest to people outside their circle. After I received this letter, I stopped polemicizing, but first I stopped wondering why *Tygodnik Powszechny* was no longer interesting.

The main danger I saw to literature and culture was the

beginning of an attempt to subordinate literature by imposing this or that canon; for me, literature has value only when it judges its permanence in terms broader than immediate historical aims and, preserving its deep human sense, is not subject to this or that passing tactical postulate. I understood that these postulates were variable and underwent several modifications, that they were tested by various circumstances, and since I believed that literature should never have to submit to these modifications, I also believed that it should not become part of the power apparatus. On the contrary, I thought that a critical literature would be the greatest asset to society, a literature which every authority would have to take into account and always has taken into account since the State and literature began. Because literature is created with a view to history; it is as though its task were to evaluate reality and each authority had to take this test into account. I thought and I still think that literature is society's court of appeals and that, in recognition of their best interests, the governed and the governing should allow this court to retain the rights which belong to it and which it has earned through the ages.

A very important problem at the time was the new literary generation. I knew that the circumstances in which this generation was shaped had been very difficult. I also realized that in the conditions which then prevailed it was easy for irresponsible demagogues to enmesh the young literary generation in a web of platitudes and turn it against the group of older writers who had a clearer view of the true tasks of literature. Believing that it was improper under any circumstances to engage in open controversy with our younger colleagues and that those who really had something to say sooner or later would understand that subordinating literature to the immediate requirements of authority would nullify literature by depriving it of the possibility of critical evaluation and society of the element of necessary criticism, and lead to the moral nihilism of the rulers and the ruled — believing all this, I steered clear of any kind of controversy and did not join the literary youth organization. I thought that the aversion and mockery which the young felt for the older generation were the natural rights of youth and I feared only the exploitation of these natural rights by people whose aims did not include the good of Polish literature.

The "model" of Russian literature was another essential problem, which forced its way bit by bit into our polemics. During my involuntary stay in Russia, I had acquired a rather thorough knowledge of Russian literature and history. Even before this, Dostoevsky and Tolstoy had been my favorite writers, as I previously had become acquainted with their works in Polish and French translations. But I never had any doubt that the greatness of these writers and the outstanding merits of many other Russian authors of the nineteenth century were directly connected with the evolution of historical conditions in Russia; that classical Russian literature had developed against the background of Russian life and the extremely difficult, complex, conscience-tormenting conditions of this life. I believed also that the great, long traditions of Polish literature—whose lines of development run along a different route, through medieval Latin, the humanism of the Golden Age, the rationalism of the Enlightenment, and the hundred-year period of struggle for national independence, and are connected as well with the great cultural traditions of antiquity, Christian universalism and the living and continuous process of cultural exchange—were strong enough to allow the shaping of new cultural values consistent with the tradition of Polish humanism, and that, as a result of the new social transformation they would embrace the broad ranks of the nation. I believed, and I still believe, that in a country with a thousand-year-old cultural tradition, new cultural values would arise in the new historical period, and that there was no reason to call for a search for any kind of model, including the model of Soviet literature, which for many years has not fulfilled the demands that could be made of it by readers of Dostoevsky, Tolstoy and other Russian prose writers and poets whose names not so long ago were eliminated from the official history of literature. I understood that "socialist realism" had its roots in Belinski's thesis on the role of art, according to which a philosopher and an artist differ only in their way of expressing themselves. This thesis was shaped during the corresponding period of Russian history and can be applied only to the prose of novelists.

But it is difficult, after more than a hundred years, in another country, and in altogether different circumstances—in the period when artistic investigation must be limited on the basis of experience to certain periods and genres—to accept the resurrection of Belinski's thesis and to transplant it mechanically onto the ground of our literature and science of literature. Moreover, it wasn't so long ago that, as a result of the special interpretation of the writer's role, the aim of literature was to project a fictitious reality and present it to the reader for study. "Socialist realism" was proclaimed under these conditions: the progressive Stalinization of the socialist process in Poland, accompanied by the cult of unconditional authority, complete subordination of all streams of social life to the State and Party administration, and the thorough bureaucratization of cultural life. The Szczecin Rally, at which the whole system of prohibitions and norms for literature was proclaimed, initiated the sorry period of the devastation of Polish culture and delayed for several years its vigorous growth, which we had witnessed in the first years when arbitrary decisions did not appear with the force they acquired after 1949.

But, to keep to the chronological order, I must go back to my first effort to polemicize with a bureaucracy which was taking over the leading positions in culture. This bureaucracy established itself not outside but within the literary milieu. It was noticeable at first on the editorial boards of periodicals, where there was always someone elected by dark forces to decide all matters, including the question of publishing a certain article or a certain author; it also made itself felt in publishing houses, where editors and section chiefs meekly submitted to reviewers and policymakers forsworn by the same bureaucratic forces. It must be said that many of these bureaucratic representatives were recruited from among the writers themselves or from among the broad ranks of quasi-litterateurs and columnists who somewhere, sometime, had published something, who had good visas on their political passports and who, as a result of these two facts, had acquired the certificate of cultural specialists. These people, often gifted, having taste and some knowledge, placed no value on the humanistic role of literature, were indifferent to the problem of national culture, and knew only that they had to execute the orders of their bureaucratic superiors. Indeed, they fulfilled their duty conscientiously, and in this way fortified, on the one hand, their authority as "connoisseurs" and, on the other, acquired, in editorial offices, publishing houses and later in the organized life of the Writers' Union, the stature of grey eminences.

So the first experiment I tried in a timid attempt to oppose the imposition of false doctrines decidedly failed. Specifically, in 1948, I tried to publish a short article on the problem of the relationship between creator and agent, believing, and I think not without reason, that this was a very appropriate matter for discussion. This article, set in type and approved for publication in the later suspended *Nowiny Literackie*, only to be deleted at the last moment by the editor, I read without any changes to the Eleventh Cultural Council in 1954. To the unchanged script I added only a few introductory sentences which corroborated the sad state of Polish literature. This speech, which the editors shortened only by these few introductory sentences, appeared in *Przeglad Kulturalny*, April 22-28 of the same year. The grey eminences failed to notice in the same issue of *Nowiny Literackie* a short poem entitled, "From the Workshop of a Modern Poet," which touched on the same subject, only more generally and in the spirit of poetry.

The first sharp skirmish came in 1949. I published in *Kuznica*, No. 18, an editorial called "Notes About a Book" which dealt with the importance of books in shaping modern humanistic culture in Poland. I had always been interested in publishing, which seemed to me to be a crucially important field. I believed that it was not the literary periodicals or our polemics, but publishing policies that primarily would determine the character of the new reader's mind. A whole generation reared in wartime and occupation had been denied the normal flow of information; the deficiencies in the education of youth were terrifying. I had the opportunity to convince myself of this in 1948, when as a member of the examining committee I tested several scores of candidates for university entrance. The unbelievable simplicity of their minds, the vulgarization of political content, the justified fear and passivity on the part of former teachers, the lack of preparation and experience of young teachers—all this did not augur well for the intellectual character of the new generation beginning work on its own. In view of these conditions, and the flood of "simplified literature," domestic and translated, I thought that the proper publishing policy would be to give the fullest possible representation to classical Polish and foreign literature; I believed that this material would provide a base from which it would be possible to create new reading tastes and, what is more important, a yardstick by which the new reader could judge what was and was not of humanistic value in the new literature.

I consciously counterpoised the naive, shortsighted writing demanded by the bureaucracy against the lasting values of Polish classics and foreign literature. Then, I was struck by a thunderbolt, in the form of an article meaningfully entitled: "The Struggle of Classes or Tastes" (Kuznica, No. 24). This was already after the Szczecin Rally, where urbi et orbi, "socialist realism" had been proclaimed as the only correct and possible literary doctrine. For the members of Kuznica, this was also after an unexpected change had been made in the post of managing editor. In a reply to my article, the new managing editor called my outlook "Girondist"—which for those in the know was obviously a euphemism. Even at the time, I had no chance to argue; besides, I had become more and more convinced that there was no possibility of discussion. The new course proclaimed for literature was a theoretical blind which the Stalinist bureaucracy used to control the writer's conscience.

Soon an organizational maneuver, fatal in its consequences, was effected: namely, several periodicals were liquidated and two were merged—*Kuznica* and *Odrodzenie*. Before this happened, I was kicked off *Kuznica*'s editorial staff where, until then, and with tremendous difficulty, I had run the press review column.

Shortly after the Szczecin Rally, changes were made in the organizational structure of the Writers' Union, which became one of the tools to keep disobedient literature in line. Literature became completely subordinated to bureaucracy. I felt that, in such a situation, there was nothing to do but find some sort of work which would allow me to keep my integrity and would not create occasion for a conflict whose outcome could have only one meaning—work which would not force me to declare my allegiance to principles I did not recognize, because they negated Polish cultural traditions and needs and had nothing in common with the humanistic content of the social changes which, to my mind, were right and which, in the first three years after the war, I had tried to further with all my knowledge and ability.

I busied myself with editing books, I corrected Polish translations of Russian classics, and I made translations myself. The result was a compendium of the translated works of Tolstoy and Turgenev, the first new translations of Dostoevsky, my own translations of Tolstoy and Turgenev, my contribution to the theoretical works of the PEN Club, an essay on the tradition of Polish translations and, finally, several years' work in the Writers' Union on organizational matters connected with this field. As is known, the Writers' Union was reorganized after the Szczecin Rally and, instead of being a professional organization, became an educational-rallying institution, whose task was to check the fidelity to the principles of "socialist realism" at its interminable sectional meetings. I had been against the sectional structure from the very beginning, believing that this medieval breakdown of writers along lines of literary specialization was absurd, and that all discussions and criticism should be conducted in the columns of literary periodicals. The fact that literary life retired behind the walls of the house of the dead, as I called the location of the Writers' Union, could only help the bureaucracy, which codified the norms of literary life there, distributing kisses and slaps as if it were a Victorian boarding school for girls. To use the vocabulary of "ferdydurkism" which then governed Polish life everywhere, I must say that we became completely stultified. The time of the "long, soul-searching night conversations" began. The big test of human character also began, as well as the lesson in morality and logic.

I tried, using the method of ducking—the only right one at this time—to speedily isolate myself from the literary milieu and at the same time to work most efficiently wherever it was possible to do so without compromising myself or my own creative ability. I believed it would be socially useful to occupy myself with translations and that this would undoubtedly give me personal satisfaction as well. I believed also, that it was necessary to help the great and useful group of translators whose output in those sad years of 1949-1953, along with the conscientiously edited and published editions of the classics, assured the whole new generation of readers an appropriate yardstick.

In organizational work, I tried my best to divert the wave of bureaucracy from the translator's section, where I was a board member for several years; but there also I soon encountered friction. This time, the reasons for it were material matters. Namely, new rules were voted which put the translators in a very difficult position and in circumstances immeasurably worse than those of their other colleagues. The rules were introduced against the publishers' advice on the motion of one of the Union's delegates. It seemed nonsensical to me that the board of directors had to act in a way that was harmful to the members; aside from this, the affair had a wider scope and was linked with such important problems as the state of literary translations, the quality and standard of translations, and the influx of young translators into the small group of specialists. There was an unpleasant uproar at one of the section meetings when the Union's Secretary General arrived. His sharp intervention did not change our stand in this matter which, unfortunately, despite some few changes for the good, hasn't been settled properly today. But at the time, in the far-advanced atmosphere of suspicion and spreading fear, the incident with the translators had its meaning. It is sad today to think that such petty and obvious matters could have become the reason for a split of ranks along two distinct and contradictory lines. But it was so at the time. The atmosphere of gloom, evoked by drilling writers ceaselessly, admonishing them, using open threats, constantly identifying any non-conformity in thinking with hostility, qualifying opposition in cultural and theoretical matters by paragraphs of the criminal code—all this, to the accompaniment of an increasing number of political trials and a mounting wave of arrests, silenced the literary group. The paradoxical situation arose in which ardent speakers at rallies and conventions would inveigh against their own interpretation of the ideas of their silent opponents.

Today, when I ask myself whether only the advocates of "socialist realism"—which, I repeat, in my opinion was nothing but a theoretical screen behind which the trustees of the administration could strangle any thought in the way of the Stalinist bureaucrats—were responsible for all that was our lot in those years, the answer is no.

Speaking at the Eleventh Cultural Council, I used a form of expression which, at the time, was repeated in the lobbies and afterwards appeared in the columns of the press. This was a short parable addressed to the then Secretary General of the Writers' Union, and its moral was that, if someone asks me to perform a certain job which goes against my conscience and understanding of common sense, then the fault lies not only with the person who gives the order but also with the person who executes it—which means me. The Secretary General of the Writers' Union was offended by this parable, in which he was represented as the order-giver. I would like to comfort him here by saying that he also could have invented some kind of parable and addressed it afterwards to one of his own order-givers. And the fact that he did not do that probably meant that he agreed with the orders he had received. But, as I have always thought, the drill system is especially difficult to apply to artists. An adult man is a man who thinks and acts independently. Independence and the sense of responsibility that results from it—these are the things which primarily characterize an artist. The whole risk of choice and all its consequences must be borne by the artist alone. And nobody can help him or substitute for him in this. So any kind of system of drill, orders, warnings or threats addressed to the artist which somehow implies a division of responsibility in taking the risk of choice makes any kind of artistic work impossible. One must remember that no artist was ever subjected to the kind of organizational restrictions that have occurred in our political system. Therefore the organizers of social life are advised to take painstaking care in their work so as not to limit the artist's basic characteristic—full independence—and to ensure that only he takes the risk of choice and all its consequences. For the creator, such consequences should mean only this: that his work will survive or will be useless and forgotten. But the society in which and for which the artist works must be the first to make this decision. For only this society can formulate the system of prohibitions and imperatives which best expresses its national traditions and the moral sense of the artist's own generation. But often, when even these two criteria are inadequate, the artist still has the future as his court of appeals.

But to return to the question: who is guilty? It should be stated that the guilty are those who created the shortsighted system of prohibitions and commands, and those who were willing to ally themselves with the system. To speak with absolute sincerity—and today there should be no other way of speaking—there was no danger of any kind for the artist who did not care to ally himself with this system, no danger except silence. In my own experience, I don't know of a single instance when anyone forced me to write something I didn't want to write. I also don't know of any instance in which some of my work was published in changed or abridged form without my consent. Any such procedure was carried out with the author's agreement, and if he did consent he should be angry primarily with himself. So I think that the charge that there was bad writing, writing that was stupid and false, should be directed to the writers. The only essential thing is the work that wasn't created, the books we didn't write, the problems we didn't solve, the intellectual theories we didn't advance, for all this, undoubtedly hindered the development of literature and impoverished the moral and intellectual life of the nation. And how, in this light, does the question of responsibility appear? In my opinion, the responsibility falls on those who, in 1949, openly and brutally created an intellectual and artistic atmosphere which not only made it impossible to publish the results of the writers' creative work, but first annihilated any spirit for this work and spread nihilism and the feeling of helplessness.

Without surprise and without bitterness, I have come across statements in which I find something of an apology for accepting this atmosphere. Those who think this way were sure that such and no other was "historical necessity" and that they should have allied themselves with this "necessity." If they believe this, that is their business. Just as no instrument exists which would verify the sincerity of their not-so-old enthusiasm for depicting the pretenses of Polish life, so there is also no instrument which would allow us to measure the depth of their conviction of the "historical necessity" for submission. I repeat: a writer is independent and he alone takes the risk of choice. It is difficult to agree when those same writers today ask us still to award them the lead in infallibility and the diploma for continuous leadership of literary affairs.

As I have said, at no time was I forced to write anything I didn't want to write. Throughout this period, only once and of my own free will did I betray my convictions, and I should like to make a note of this.

In 1952, on the day before one of those consecutive plenary sessions of the Union at which "rules" were set, it was proposed that I and one of my colleagues who, like me, had not published his work for a long time, should publish articles in the official periodical of the Writers' Union. This was obviously intended to offset the impression that there existed formerly active writers who were now being denied the possibility of publication. It was also aimed at discrediting notions that some kind of opposition existed. I refer here to only two of us, though perhaps others also were involved. But my very limited connections with the literary entourage at the time made it impossible for me to verify this. So I, and my colleague, who is an outstanding critic, decided that this proposition somehow gave us the right of combatants and we agreed to take advantage of it. I realized that in the sketch I intended to publish I would have to express my opinion on "socialist realism." Therefore, in this essay, which was on literary criticism and its attitude toward writing, I wrote some ten sentences in which I detached myself from the literary practice of "socialist realism" and discussed its theoretical possibilities. I must confess that when I read these lines in print, I came to the conclusion that the game wasn't worth it, and that all halfway solutions would lead me to the place I didn't wish to reach. So, after that, I never made use of my limited rights as a combatant.

The greatest evil inflicted on Polish culture in those years was implanting in us the conviction that all discussion was futile. The process of patterning intellectual life on Byzantine obscurantism was carried to the extreme, so that even the shadow of a critical thought vanished in the limelight of inevitable approbation, in the soulless monotony of those complicated pronouncements which began with "even if so" and "therefore" and were followed by superlatives and exaltation. It was necessary to call on one's patience and forbearance not to submit to this painful atmosphere, to the tragic conviction of the "historical necessity" for hypocrisy, flattery and lies.

Some, to justify their conformity, recalled the court literatures, forgetting that Horace did not glorify Augustus only, that Ovid wrote his *Tristia* in exile, that Racine wrote about kings but not for kings, that Shakespeare was unimpressed by the ways of the court, and that Russian literature of the nineteenth century, subjected to stupid censorship, was boundlessly free compared with ours in the years between 1949 and 1953.

From 1949 to 1953, I wrote very little and published even less, not because I had nothing to say, but because I couldn't write about the things that interested me most. I couldn't write about freedom of conscience, about the attitude of the rulers towards the ruled, about the falseness of "historical necessity," about the right of the individual man to protest, about the abuse of power, the neglect of national tradition, and the one-sided, faulty interpretation of solidarity in international affairs. The roster of these things is unending. Indeed, a writer couldn't touch on one basic problem, and therefore the literature of those times was worthless; even if in particular cases a writer created a work commensurate with his talent, it always failed to come up to the intellectual requirements of the reader, who was not bound by the system of prohibition and command proclaimed in Szczecin and developed later in the literary press and innumerable Union sessions. Then came what is always the worst for literature—and fatal for writers. Literature lost its moral and intellectual prestige and the writer lost the confidence of his own society.

Between 1949 and 1953, I wrote a score of verses and

several score pages of prose. These were critical and literary sketches, short essays published as feuilletons in the daily press and afterwards in the form of a small book, which gained me the friendship of readers. During this time, I thought over various matters, particularly the fate of Polish literature and, above all, of poetry. I tried to grasp the difference between the folk and the national, to find that mysterious moment when the full and vulgar melody becomes part of the national harmony. These thoughts resulted in a short poem which summed up my experience in this matter. In this period, I also had occasion to become acquainted with the concept of Polish literature prepared by the bureaucracy. Namely, I wrote an essay on one of the unjustly forgotten Polish poets of the nineteenth century whose fineness and sad resignation moved me at the time. Oddly enough, this essay gave rise to a violent dispute among the young literary historians. I came to the conclusion that the practice of subordinating the study of literature to immediate political aims was as ruthless as subordinating literature itself. What was more astonishing was that those who were experts in literary history, and who called themselves Marxists, neglected in their work on nineteenth century Polish writing so essential an aspect as the struggle for independence, and emphasized the theme of social emancipation, as if these two things could be separated. Here, as in the theory of literature, the official interpretation of the revolutionary thesis of Russian democrats of the nineteenth century was accepted as the final word, a fact which in a field clearly concerned with the history of our own literature produced the most pitiful results.

The first overt sign of protest on my part, or to be precise, the documentation of my protest against this state of affairs, encompassing a much larger sphere than literature and the history of literature, was published in a series of verses in *Tworczosc*, March 1955. I mention this, because the verses provoked a sharp reaction from the bureaucratic plenipotentiaries of literature. Compared with the works later published by my friends, these verses were innocent, but at the time they were considered a mark of offense. At one of the Union's successive sessions, a young critic, who could not even list among his achievements a few pages of published criticism, was authorized by the elder plenipotentiaries, distributing the inevitable slaps and kisses, to read aloud those incriminating verses as an example of my ideological downfall. But these were no longer the old days, and the audience responded with applause.

I will remember this applause. Not because it was for my poetry. I had been applauded and blamed more than once. I will remember this applause because, for the first time in many long years, there was a public expression of contempt for the policy of slaps and kisses used against authors. And although my verses are certainly inferior to everything that was written afterwards with so much beauty and audacity, they cannot be denied this precedence.

From 1955 on, the "night conversations" began to appear in the columns of periodicals, at first unsure of themselves and later more and more bold. It seemed to me that I would be able to return to the normal work of a writer, as I had after the war. But it became evident that a long silence has a devastating effect. You must put your thoughts in order and reconsider the future.

I realized personally that in cultural matters one of the most important things is to recover the norms proper to civilized principles of organized cultural life. Perhaps the problem of organization would not be so essential if it were not for the fact that through it and with its help a vacuum was created in our life. The forms of organization would be unimportant if it were not for the fact that so long as they exist there will always be some eager ones who will profit from their existence and start organizing a new system of prohibitions and orders, a new apparatus for the distribution of slaps and kisses.

The necessity of reshaping the present structure of the Union and reorganizing cultural life is universally understood today. Evidence of this was the Eleventh Cultural Council and the open session of the Party organization of the Polish Writers' Union, where I stated, among other things, that:

"Our rally is taking place after the first period of important changes in public opinion. Precisely speaking, after the first period in which public opinion was expressed in an open and uncompromising manner and became outspoken about many things which until now have been veiled in a conspiracy of silence. What happened last month was not for everyone, what one of our Cracow colleagues called, 'an earthquake.' For many people in Poland, regardless of the character of their occupation and the differences in their outlook, this thing that happened was the obvious result of an old truth, the profound folk and universal truth that methods cannot be contrary to purposes, and that the Jesuitical principle of the end justifying the means must be cast out of a program based on principles of humanism and common sense.

"Indeed, in the course of the past years, we had to deal with a specific form of Jesuitry which allowed no shade of criticism, which stated that good was evil and evil, good, and that only through this reversal of the order of things would we achieve eternal happiness. It is necessary to add that it was a special kind of Jesuitry, reinforced by Talmudism and the primitive belief in totems and taboos.

"Obviously, this whole system—which, for the average citizen, was manifested flagrantly in economic conditions, in obvious ways such as the squandering of public money, the famous Byzantine character of our architecture, the mass meetings which lasted for many hours and inevitably ended in beating the same tune to so-called spontaneous applause, etc.—this whole system was reflected in our work even more concretely and, it must be said, more dangerously.

"I do not overestimate the immediate impact of the printed word, nor do I imagine that the mere statement of one formula or another can have a direct influence on anything, especially when the formula is the intellectual proposition of a writer or columnist who has no executive power behind him or administrative machine at his disposal. But when the situation is reversed, when the writer has no opportunity to make any kind of intellectual proposition, when all that is left to him is the right to repeat someone else's propositions, which have already been reinforced besides by a tremendous power apparatus and administration—then creators are morally and intellectually sterilized and society is forced to turn its back on them in indifference or, what is worse, in scorn. But while it is possible to forbid writers to print their work, you cannot forbid people to think.

"It is necessary to say here that this process of separating literature from the essential requirements and opinions of society, which was defined after the Szczecin Convention, was halted in its development, thanks to the activity of writers, columnists, orators and many Polish men of letters; it is not necessary to mention their names here. We know them very well. This process, which we refer to euphemistically as schematism or varnishing, alarmed not only those who saw its full danger, but even those who, with an eagerness befitting a better cause, tried in the beginning to impose it on our literature. This is neither the time nor the place to mention the names of those writers who inaugurated this process outside the literary milieu. In this process of generally revising our views, it must be kept in mind that literary life in this period was subjected not only to the pressure of the administration from outside but also, and above all, to pressure from the inside. The walls of the assembly room of the Writers' Union and the walls of other less important rooms in this beautiful building, could tell us many a thing. It is also obvious that efforts to refrain from schematism, varnishing and simplifying—to readjust literary life when it became obvious that the Szczecin theory and the post-Szczecin practice had led to catastrophe—could not be successful. First, because these efforts were centered only and exclusively on the manner of execution. There was sharp criticism of the dullness, intellectual poverty, moral vacuity and primitive naivete of many works, but there was never any attempt to peer into the causes of such phenomena which, if only because of their universality, were unusual in the literature of a nation of twenty-seven million people and with a thousand years of culture and history. At the very time when literary historians had no trouble in defining the causes for the downfall of writing in Poland's Saxon dynasty period, the critics were somehow unable to spot the real causes for the decay of literature in our own time.

"Indeed, it wasn't easy; indeed, it wasn't possible at all. It wasn't possible because of various considerations, i.e. — one could not have declared that the thesis that the class struggle increases as socialism advances was incorrect and led to terrible results. In fact, recognition of this theory alone makes intellectual activity impossible, particularly in literature, which is not and cannot be anything other than a constant struggle to express one's thoughts about everything around us and within us more perfectly. As is known within us and around us, and as the essence of life and literature shows, there were and will be many individual thoughts, personal, separate, and often different from the formula of this or that stage, not only in our books or articles but also in our political pamphlets.

"All these efforts to cure literature which were nevertheless sometimes made, were destined to fail. Indeed, they were nothing but formalism a rebours and, as we know, dealt with the manner of execution and not with the heart of the matter.

"It seems to me that the history of the past years taught us precisely that any kind of attempt to administer literature and to direct it leads to the failure of literature and the collapse of its social importance. It is necessary to say that the present structure of literary life gives us no assurance that this state of affairs will change. In every politico-social formation, essential changes must be accompanied by adequate and successive organizational changes. These changes will, in turn, influence and fortify the internal changes."

The record of my outlook on contemporary literary affairs

is a letter which I sent to the editor of *Nowa Kultura* in June 1956. This letter, published in August of the same year (No. 33) is in reply to a questionnaire circulated by the editors.

It is obvious that no change in the structure of the Writers' Union, no reorganization of periodicals, and no administrative act of one kind or another will automatically change the fact that for years Polish literature has lacked truth, which the nation knows as well as the authors. It will be possible to regain the reader's confidence only when there are works which give deep artistic value to everything we are chaotically and fervently saying today, when the lights and shadows are artistically composed into pictures. This will take conscience and courage on the part of writers whose task is to tell not only what they see and know, but first of all, what they think about what is known and seen. The condition for true literary development will be, therefore, the creation of a moral and intellectual atmosphere in which each of us in his own way will be willing to say what he thinks. For what is needed is not only officially proclaimed freedom but real freedom, which can result only from the structure of national life. For despite the fact that I emphasize the matter of the organization of literary life, which in the present historical conditions can and should support everything that assures this freedom—the basic guarantee I see is the awakened social consciousness of the masses and the open character of public life. But a change in organizational forms is important insofar as that even today, the supporters of yesterday, not at all taken aback, say: let's begin anew, now after these experiences, we promise you that we will be better at organizing. We will slightly alter the principle of distributing kisses and slaps and everything will be all right. The past—it was historical necessity.

Everything I have written is part of an experiment to express thoughts which today come chaotically, and stormily, and will not compose themselves into a harmonious picture. There is no way in these recollections to separate the personal from the general. The writer can rely only on himself. But in his isolation he always bears in mind that everything he thinks and does will find its ultimate shape in the work he gives to the world. And in the end, the world decides the value of our solitary nights and days, in which we can rely only on ourselves, on our own understanding of good and evil, truth and falsehood, beauty and ugliness. No one can do our work for us, and today or tomorrow, someone who has been given the ability to express his view of this world and his own thoughts about it, will settle down to write a book in which all this tremendous chaos of suffering, humility, bitterness and hope that we share will be composed into a grave and wise judgment of the world and the time in which we happen to live.

Translated by Zygmunt Haupt

Leszek Kolakowski

Permanent and Transitory Aspects of Marxism[1]

The Greatest Philologist in the World announced in a monumental work published in a daily newspaper[2] that Marr's theory of language was false. It happened that only a few days later I had an opportunity to attend a discussion by a group of philologists on this very subject. During the discussion one of the participants rather tactlessly produced a pamphlet published several weeks earlier by one of the philologists present, and quoted a passage which read roughly as follows: "It is quite obvious that in linguistics Marr's theory is the only genuine Marxist-Leninist theory of language; this theory alone is fully compatible with the principles of Marxism-Leninism; this particular theory is an infallible instrument in Marxist-Leninist linguistic research, etc." Then the malicious fellow produced the current issue of the above-men-

[1] This essay was published in the Warsaw literary weekly *Nowa Kultura*, January 27, 1957.
[2] See Stalin's articles on Marxism in linguistics, first published in *Pravda*, June 22, 1950.

157

tioned daily and quoted a fragment from an article by the same author. It read approximately as follows: "It is obvious that Marr's theory has nothing in common with Marxism-Leninism; it is a strikingly vulgar parody of Marxism-Leninism; the Marxist-Leninist conception of language must be firmly opposed to Marr's theory, etc."

"What is the meaning of such a reversal in only a few weeks?" cried the critic indignantly. "What a chameleon!"

The author of the quoted passage, confused, remained silent. Everybody laughed merrily until a party activist, present at the meeting, spoke up and pointed out that the merriment was entirely uncalled for. After all, a man has a right to change his opinions, and that in itself should not be considered a disgrace.

As I listened, my first impression was that the critic had been right when he embarrassed the philologist by showing up his intellectual opportunism and his shameful readiness to reverse his opinion with lightning speed in order to conform to the judgment delivered by the Greatest Philologist in the World. Only later, much later, did I realize that it was the embarrassed author of the pamphlet who was the genuine Marxist, whereas his critic had shown himself to be completely ignorant. Because—and here is the heart of the matter and the main problem I want to consider—Marr's theory was *truly* in agreement with Marxism two days before the publication of the Greatest Philologist's work, and became *truly* incompatible with Marxism on the day this work appeared. Since the author of the pamphlet was a genuine Marxist he had no reason to be ashamed, but ought to have prided himself on his unshakeable faithfulness to the principles of Marxism.

Principles? Perhaps this is not a good choice of words. The point is that the term "Marxism" did not designate a doctrine with a specific content. It meant a doctrine defined only formally, its content being, in each case, supplied by the Infallible Institution. During a certain phase this institution was the Greatest Philologist, the Greatest Philosopher, the

Greatest Economist and the Greatest Historian in the World.

In short, "Marxism" became a concept of institutional rather than intellectual import—which, by the way, happens to every doctrine connected with a church. Similarly, the word "Marxist" does not describe a man who believes in a world view defined by a given content. It refers to a man with a mental attitude characterized by his willingness to accept institutionally-approved opinions. From this point of view the content of Marxism at a given moment does not matter. A man is a Marxist if he is always ready to accept as the content of the doctrine that which is recommended by the "Office." This is why, until February 1956,[3] the only real Marxist (which also means a revolutionary, a dialectician, a materialist) was one who agreed that there was no other way to socialism than through revolutionary violence; while in fact an anti-Marxist (that is, a reformist, a metaphysician, an idealist) was one who thought that other ways could be found. As we know, after February 1956, the reverse became true: the only real Marxist is one who recognizes that in certain countries the possibility of a peaceful transition to socialism does exist. It is difficult to predict accurately who will, with respect to this problem, be a Marxist next year. We will not be the ones to decide—the Office will settle the matter.

It is precisely for this reason, because of the institutional rather than intellectual character of Marxism, that a true Marxist will profess beliefs which he does not necessarily understand. The 1950 Marxist knows that Lysenko's theory of heredity is correct, that Hegel represented an aristocratic reaction to the French Revolution, that Dostoevsky was nothing but decadence and Babayevsky a great writer, that Suvorov served the cause of progress, and also that the resonance theory in chemistry is reactionary nonsense. Every 1950 Marxist knows these things, even if he has never learned what chromosomes are, has no idea in which century Hegel lived, never read one of Dostoevsky's books, or studied a high

---

[3] Date of the Twentieth Congress of the Communist Party of the Soviet Union.

school chemistry textbook. To a Marxist all this is absolutely unnecessary so long as the content of Marxism is determined by the Office.

In this way the concept of Marxism was defined very precisely, without any possibility of error, although the definition was purely formal in character: that is, it merely indicated where to look for the present content of Marxism, without actually specifying this content.

This appears to be chronologically the second concept of Marxism. The original one simply meant those views and theories characteristic of Karl Marx. That first, historical concept of Marxism still retains its validity and precision (in the same sense as the concept of "Platonism," "Freudianism," or "Cartesianism"), irrespective of whether any Marxist — meaning in this context a believer in Marx's views—exists in the world.

We are thus faced with a question: if the sort of Marxism in which the doctrinal content was periodically established by the Office is now dead in the minds of the majority of intellectuals who considered themselves Marxists, has the concept of Marxism retained any meaning at all? If so, what meaning other than the historical one which has to do with the work of a man whose name is now connected with a doctrine? What meaning have the slogans urging the "development of Marxism," and what meaning is left in the distinction between Marxists and non-Marxists in science?

Before the Office was born, and with it the new concept of Marxism, the answer to this question was not a very difficult one. Outstanding theoreticians—Russian revolutionaries like Lenin, Trotsky, or Bukharin—when analyzing, for example, the social situation and history of Russia, applied a conceptual framework built by Marx to situations which Marx himself never considered; they operated with the Marxist concept of class, which was no doubt a theoretical novelty that distinguished it from other doctrines, and utilized it to describe the relation of forces in Russian society. Here it is clear what is meant by developing Marxism: the application of Marx's method and conceptual apparatus to new subjects of study. Let us suppose, however, that certain social processes arise for which this conceptual apparatus is no longer adequate. It is possible to admit that this apparatus is adequate when applied to the capitalist societies so thoroughly analyzed by Marx, and also to recognize the accuracy of these analyses, while at the same time maintaining that this conceptual scheme is not applicable to the study of new, non-capitalist societies where new concepts must be used to analyze basic social stratification. (This problem is discussed, among others, by Stanislaw Ossowski[4] in his still unpublished work *Approaches to the Problem of Class Structure in Social Consciousness*, which I had an opportunity to see in manuscript form.) Can the attempt to build such a new conceptual scheme aspire to be called "Marxist"? It is contradictory to Marxism, therefore "non-Marxist," provided we make the assumption that conceptual categories built by Marx are all that is necessary to describe and analyze every social phenomenon which might ever occur. Marx, of course, never made this assumption; it is an original contribution of his Stalinist epigoni. However, if such an attempt is merely not contradictory to Marxism, does it mean that it is "Marxist"?

One could, of course, agree on a convention to call all achievements of science and all scientific truths by the name of "Marxism." But in such a case we should have to consider as Marxist all discoveries in astrobotany, every new generalization in physiology, and every new theorem in topology. In

---

[4] Stanislaw Ossowski is a prominent Polish philosopher and sociologist, whose publications cover a wide range of subjects. (E.g., *Foundations of Aesthetics*, 1949; *Social Ties and Heredity*, 1948.) He is also the author of a few remarkable essays on Marxism, published first in 1947 in the now defunct Warsaw monthly, *Contemporary Thought*, and recently reissued (1957) as a pamphlet by the later-suppressed weekly *Po prostu*. Ossowski's views, in particular his distinction between the two incompatible social functions of the Marxist doctrine: the "religious" (in Durkheim's sense) and the theoretical one, have undoubtedly influenced Kolakowski's approach to the whole subject of his essay.

this sense of the term, sometimes specifically postulated, the word "Marxism" is completely devoid of meaning and becomes a superfluous pseudonym for the word "truth" or "scientific knowledge." This pseudonym is not only superfluous but also mystifying, because it deviously suggests that all human knowledge is either inspired by Karl Marx, or progresses only thanks to the method formulated by him and uniquely characteristic of his scientific work. And this, obviously, is false.

And yet, to return to the above-mentioned example, if we want to develop a new conceptual scheme in order to analyze social stratification in types of societies unknown to Marx, we must fall back upon a certain methodological rule. This rule is not only observed quite consistently in Marx's writing, but is applied so forcefully and universally that it is a distinctive characteristic of his work. According to this rule, all analyses of social life should proceed by looking for the basic divisions separating societies into antagonistic groups. Even if it happens that in certain societies these divisions are based on criteria other than those formulated by Marx for the bourgeois world of the nineteenth century, still the very fact of applying this extremely general rule leads the scholar to adopt a methodological standpoint distinctly characteristic of Marx's works. From this point of view it can be said that the sociological research he is engaging in is "Marxist."

It happens, however, that the progress of knowledge requires not only a larger number of conceptual tools and methodological rules than those to be found in Marx's works, but also that some of his concrete statements be revised and questioned. The Office itself at one time proclaimed that some of Engel's assumptions concerning the origin of the State were false. The Office, according to its universal rules of procedure, did not bother to justify this revision, but for the purposes of our discussion that is a matter of secondary importance. The Office also rejected Marx's thesis that it is impossible to build a socialist society in one isolated country. When Stalin came out with his concept of socialism in one country Trotsky, as an orthodox and classical Marxist, reproached him for deviating from the principles of Marxism and was in turn called an anti-Marxist by Stalin. Refraining for the moment from judging as to who was right in this dispute and whose view was verified by historical developments, it is easy to see the scholastic sterility of a dispute so conducted. When one says, as Stalin did, that the international situation has changed since Marx's time and that Marx himself recommended that the future of socialism be viewed in terms of the current situation in the international class struggle, it means that although we employ a way of thinking used by Marx, still this way of thinking is so generalized and so common to those who want to analyze reality in a rational way that it is not specifically characteristic of "Marxist" thinking. If on the other hand one maintains, as Lenin and Trotsky did, that Marx's analysis of capitalism is not obsolete in this respect, it means that we fall back on the distinguishing features of Marx's method and on concrete results of his analysis. From this point of view, although the second position may be considered a Marxist one, the first (regardless of whether it is factually true or false) is neither characteristically "Marxist" nor "anti-Marxist." This is so because, in spite of the fact that this position is obviously contradictory to the results of Marx's own research, still it is based—legitimately or not—on a rule which, even though it was actually used by Marx, is not a distinctive feature of his own work. In other cases it is possible to question some of Marx's theses from the point of view of methodological rules not only used by him, but used in a peculiar and distinctive way. This is why an analysis of such kind could be called "Marxist" in a legitimate sense of the term.

Thus we come to the formulation of the problem under discussion. The works of Marx contain a certain number of essential features—not, however, characteristic only of him and his followers—which do not suffice to distinguish a separate school of thought: a relentlessly rationalist attitude, a sense of radical criticism, a distaste for sentimentality in social research, a deterministic method. Those in the social sciences who fail to follow the above principles—as was done in notorious and egregious breach of the elementary rules of methodological rationalism by the majority of people who called themselves Marxists—are surely not Marxists. (Whereas they easily may, and did, discredit the very notion of Marxism by associating it inseparably with their own methods of thinking and with the activities of the Office. At the same time they made those who applied Marx's scientific contributions in their work ashamed of being called Marxists.) On the other hand, those who are faithful to the above principles do not thereby become Marxists, since those principles are not uniquely characteristic features of Marx's work.

However, there are certain features of Marx's work which constitute his original contribution to the development of the social sciences. In particular there are certain methodological principles enabling man to get to know and master social reality. The principle of determinism—and determinism becomes more intelligible if it is understood as a rule of thinking and not as a metaphysical theory—is certainly not specifically Marxist. This principle does not state simply that "under the same conditions the same phenomena occur," and still less that "all events are causally determined," because in such a formulation determinism becomes an empty generalization, in this form unverifiable, and therefore absolutely fruitless in scientific research. Broadly speaking, the principle of determinism requires that we try—considering the given tasks and instruments at hand—to analyze every phenomenon most thoroughly by relating it to a framework of mutual relationships of all kinds with other phenomena. On the other hand, distinctively Marxist is a certain more specific conception of determinism, as expressed by the fundamental idea of historical materialism, namely the requirement that in a genetic analysis of political institutions and various forms of social consciousness we should seek for relationships linking these with social divisions arising from the system of ownership, or more generally, from the system of productive relations. In considering the latter we should look for their connections with technical progress.

If a principle of this sort is to be scientifically useful, it has to be formulated in a general way. It is, for instance, a very bad practice to interpret the principle as holding that fundamental class structure (in Marx's sense of the term) determines unequivocally all other divisions in the social institutions and intellectual life of society throughout the entire history of mankind.

Typical for Marx is rather the tendency to emphasize those primary social divisions which are most influential in determining historical development. Also typical is Marx's awareness of the limitations and distortions imposed upon the social sciences by pressures of social conditions which shape the scientist's thinking, and Marx's struggle to do away with ideological myths in science. In former days we would never have suspected that this struggle would have to be forcefully resumed against a doctrine disguised as Marxism. Typical of Marx is a certain kind of historicism which not only does away with evaluating historical phenomena from the standpoint of a moralizer who stands guard over eternal values; which not only is based on a general principle as to the historical relativity of the subjects under study, but also on the conviction that human nature is the product of man's social history and that our entire conception of the world is "socially subjective." This means that our conception of the world is a product of social activity: material provided by reality is reorganized so as to adjust it to our biological and social orientation in the world; only a picture formed in this way remains in human minds. In this sense, then, the whole environment is a product of human activity.

Further, typical of Marx is his practical orientation in the social sciences: his selection of problems to be dealt with was determined by whether they served the cause of an egalitarian society, the cause of abolishing class divisions, and the cause of emancipating the exploited and oppressed. Typical is his conviction that, on the strength of historical law, the capitalist economy and the political rule of the bourgeoisie will inevitably change into a socialist system, and that such a transformation will take place as a result of the proletariat's coming to power. The proletariat will, in time, abolish itself as a class, which will mean the abolition of classes as such and of the State as an instrument of class rule.

And so we have an enumeration—only as an illustration, of course—of the principles and the conclusions which in the history of science are connected specifically with the name of Marx. We speak here exclusively about matters that have to do with the methodology of the social sciences, for there is no typically Marxist methodology which has affected the progress of natural sciences (with the exception of Marxist methodology in the first, "official" meaning of the word, which successfully deterred this progress).

It is not difficult to see that many of these rules have been permanently assimilated into the practicing social sciences under auspices quite independent of official Marxism and therefore considered by the Office as non-Marxist, anti-Marxist, bourgeois, and so on. Many of Marx's ideas entered the blood stream of scientific life and thus ceased to distinguish Marx—and those who regarded themselves as orthodox believers in his doctrine—from others. From this point of view, then, dividing scientists into Marxists and non-Marxists became entirely meaningless. Still, there are other important elements of Marx's method which have not become so widely accepted and at least appear to provide the basis for making such a distinction. For several reasons, however, the question is not that simple.

First of all, the word "Marxism," as it is commonly used and in its socially most widely accepted meaning, is linked with an intellectual activity that is notorious in philosophy and sociology. I have in mind Marxism in the first of the two meanings discussed above—i.e., in the institutional meaning, associated with the activity of the Office. It is obvious that no lay sociologist or philosopher with scientific aspirations has the slightest wish to have anything in common with Marxism understood in this sense, because he does not like to be accused of taking a "religious" approach. Therefore, even if his scientific work is strongly inspired by the method of thinking originated by Karl Marx, he is either very reluctant to describe his outlook as Marxism or, if he uses the term, he will always define its meaning precisely.

This is why, in order to revitalize the distinction between Marxists and non-Marxists, it will first be necessary to have a generally accepted concept of Marxism differing from the current one. The possibility of such a revision, however, depends on certain social facts. This is so because the meaning of words is a social fact, and cannot be established arbitrarily by simply declaring that we want to devote ourselves to "true" Marxism, while up till now the majority of Marxists have really been pseudo-Marxists, "Marxists" in quotation marks, etc. . . . (This explains why, speaking of intellectual Stalinism, I am not trying to present it as a sort of pseudo-Marxism in contradistinction to something called genuine Marxism. Stalinism created a socially consequential concept of Marxism conceived as an institutional and not an intellectual phenomenon, and this concept did function successfully in social life. There was only one element of confusion in it: the name of Karl Marx from which the term was originally derived. But as time goes on etymological associations disappear or at least grow fainter in the minds of people using a given term.)

In the second place, and this is even more important, outside and independently of the existence and functioning of institutional Marxism, there emerged in the social sciences a variety of conceptual categories, methodological rules and new—now highly developed—areas of research.

Therefore, from the point of view of Marxism conceived not institutionally but intellectually, there are whole areas of research where the distinction between Marxists and non-

Marxists has never become vitally important.

Of course, one should not infer from this that Marx's method would be entirely irrelevant and unable to provide a vigorous and dynamic inspiration for research in those areas. So, e.g., sociological investigations of public opinion developed almost entirely outside the sphere of influence of the Marxist tradition. Still, it is very likely that new perspectives for research could be opened if the fundamental stock of categories of this branch of sociology were enriched by introducing Marx's concept of class. In the field of logic, the tools used by semantics did not make any reference to the social aspect of meaning, and here Marx's method of analysis might perhaps contribute in many ways to the progress of research. In many fields of research, above all in political and economic history and in the history of various areas of human culture, Marx's theoretical achievements played a significantly creative role, and this in spite of institutional Marxism. Hence it would obviously be absurd, merely because of the long existence of this institutional Marxism, to advocate a return to Ranke's type of historiography, Kallenbach's history of literature, or Zeller's history of philosophy.

Finally, in the third place, it must be observed that if the decision as to whether a given theory or historical interpretation is Marxist or non-Marxist is to make any sense at all, this decision must be based on a consideration of the very general methodological assumptions used to construct this doctrine or theory. Of course, the border line between a "fact" and an "interpretation" is flexible and defies precise definition in the social sciences just as in the natural sciences. Nevertheless, there exists a great body of knowledge whose "factual" character is beyond any doubt, and to describe it as "Marxist" is nonsense.

On the other hand, the history of science teaches that problems of interpretation are never settled with any finality. The best proof of this is provided by a fact which throws doubt on the primitive belief that it is possible to attain a complete objectivity in the social sciences, namely the fact that nearly every human generation rewrites the history of the world. The remarkable thing is that this is often done successfully. And this means that the same, or nearly the same, stock of factual knowledge lends itself to a great number of well-founded and rationally justified—though radically different—interpretations. Is it worthwhile to take the trouble to determine whether they are Marxist or not, and if so, in what cases?

From the point of view of institutional Marxism the problem is clear: in 1945 the only Marxist evaluation of Hegel was expressed in the statement that Hegel was a German chauvinist, an apologist of war, an enemy of Slavic peoples and a precursor of fascism; whereas in 1954 Hegel had become an eminent dialectician and an idealist who played an important role in shaping Marx's philosophy.

From the point of view of an intellectual, not institutional, conception of Marxism, the problem is somewhat different. There is not—and there never will be—one "truly Marxist" interpretation of Stoic philosophy, or a particular interpretation of Mickiewicz's poetry which would be "the only one compatible with Marxism," etc.

It is possible to talk about interpreting Stoic philosophy with the help of general Marxist rules of historical methodology, but the same method may lead to differing results. The notion that the methodology of the social sciences might come to resemble the technique of doing logarithms, or of using a calculating machine, and thus enable us always to proceed from a given set of facts to the same unequivocally determined result, is a chimerical hope. To return to the example of Stoicism, the progress of scholarly work on Stoicism is not limited to the application of Marx's methodology. Moreover it is far from certain that even its most rigorous application would necessarily result in conclusions that are in agreement with some particular remarks of Friedrich Engels about Stoicism.

That is why to argue, as some scholars do, as to who has the exclusive privilege of using "genuine Marxism," and to try to monopolize the honorable title of "consistent" Marxist, is nothing but sterile verbalism. It can be disputed whether a given theory fulfills more or less completely the requirements of scientific thinking to which belong also—but not exclusively—the essential rules of the method worked out by Marx. These rules, however, must be of a very general nature and anyhow they do not contain any specific instructions as to how to evaluate this or that historical phenomenon. Moreover, they lend themselves to many possible interpretations: the rule of historical materialism alone does not determine the type, form and intensity of the influence exerted by the sum total of material conditions of life on the social thought of people in all historical epochs. And, a fortiori, historical materialism does not determine whether, for example, Pascal's philosophy is to be taken as an expression of the decadent tendencies of declining feudal lords, or as representative of bourgeois thought, or something else again.

In sociological investigations, and even more so in philosophical ones, there is hardly a single unambiguous term. All assertions in a doctrine fall heir to this terminological ambiguity, even the most fundamental ones, and none of them can be accepted as absolutely precise. If terms such as "matter," "social consciousness," "knowledge," "superstructure," "causal determination," "relations of production," etc., are not clear, it follows that no methodological rule nor any assertion of the theory in which they are used have a clearly defined meaning.

Therefore, what is called Marxism, as understood in its intellectual function and as a method of thinking, may vary greatly in content within the limits of a very general framework. No doubt it would hardly be possible to develop a Marxist angelology, or to consider Bossuet's philosophy of history as Marxist. To know this, however, is not very useful since our primary purpose in employing the term "Marxism" is not to distinguish scientific thinking from the obvious irrationalism of theologians. The fact is that within the boundaries of science various styles of thinking and various types of methodology can very well coexist and compete among themselves, and consequently the borderline between Marxism and non-Marxism is very fluid.

It is obvious that it cannot be otherwise in view of the aforementioned facts, namely that the rules formulated by Marx do not in themselves suffice for contemporary scholarly work, and that they do not have clearly defined meaning. Moreover, the limits of their validity are fluid. Thus to speak of a "compact and uniform Marxist camp," in contradistinction to the rest of the world, determining by its very existence a basic line of division in science, or to proclaim shibboleths about the "purity" of Marxist doctrine—all this makes no sense to the intellectual conception of Marxism. It may have a certain utility, but only when Marxism is considered as a political or religious phenomenon rather than a science.

In circumstances where we must venture to separate knowledge from faith, as the Averroists did against orthodoxy in the thirteenth century, as politics becomes less able to compromise the content of scientific knowledge, the Marxist "camp" in science will lose its former monolithic shape and grow more and more tenuous. Of course, the tradition of the old rigid division into Marxists and non-Marxists is not defunct and will certainly exert pressure on scientific life for a long time to come, even in places where institutional Marxism is dead and discredited in the social consciousness. It is equally certain, however, that the pressure of this tradition will continue to decrease along with the gradual elimination of institutional Marxism from the realm of science.

This, of course, is not to imply that in the social sciences and humanities, where the influence of social conditions is greatest, all divisions resulting from differing world views will disappear. But the most significant division is not that between orthodox Marxists guarding the purity of the doctrine against any admixture of heathen blood, on the one hand, and everyone else on the other. The most significant division—to use political language for a moment—is the division between Right and Left in the social sciences. This division is characterized not so much by a difference in methodology as by a difference in intellectual attitudes.

By the intellectual Left in the social sciences we understand the intellectual activity distinguished by: radical rationalism in thinking; resistance to any invasion of myth in scientific work; an entirely non-religious view of the world; radical criticism; distrust of all closed doctrines and systems; striving for open-mindedness, i.e., readiness to revise accepted theses, theories and methods; positive attitude toward original thinking in science; and tolerance for differing scientific standpoints, together with simultaneous readiness to oppose and even to attack every type of irrationalism. This intellectual Left is further characterized by its belief in the cognitive value of science and its conviction that social progress is possible.

Like all classifications, this one is not definitive in the way that national boundaries are. Still it seems to me to be incomparably more significant than the classification traditionally accepted in the Marxist camp. Wherever these attitudes exist, they constitute a sufficient guarantee that all the scientific contributions of Karl Marx—the importance of which for the social sciences and humanities cannot be overrated—will be preserved and made a permanent element of scientific thought. These attitudes make it possible to decide what is obsolete in Marx's doctrine and what is unfounded generalization, disproved by subsequent history. For today it is quite clear that several of Marx's ideas, in particular his predictions as to the further course of historical development, did not survive the merciless test of time. This also applies to many other prophecies. These mistaken ideas of Marx retain their significance only as utopias, as moral stimuli, rather than scientific theory.

Moreover, we can assume that with the gradual refinement of research techniques in the social sciences and humanities, the concept of Marxism as a separate school of thought will gradually become blurred and ultimately disappear entirely. (There is no "Newtonism" in physics, no "Linneism" in botany, no "Harveyism" in physiology, and no "Gaussism" in mathematics.) This implies that what is permanent in Marx's work will be assimilated in the natural course of scientific development. In the process some of his theses will be restricted in scope, others will be more precisely formulated, still others will be discarded.

But the greatest triumph of an eminent scholar comes precisely when his achievements cease to be a separate school of thought; when they melt into the very tissue of scientific life and become an elemental part of it, losing in the process their separate existence. This process is, of course, different and much slower in the social sciences and humanities, but even there it is an essential part of progress.

It is otherwise in the field of philosophy, looked upon as a discursive expression of the *Weltanschauung*. Names of great creative philosophers live through the centuries in the names of trends and schools of thought, which however, may change their character. When we use the term "Platonism" to describe a particular contemporary tendency in philosophy, we do not refer to orthodox believers in the whole Platonic doctrine, because they do not exist. "Platonism" in the current philosophical context refers only to a more or less distant affinity with those ideas of Plato which have survived as the most characteristic feature of his thought: belief in the primacy of the species over the individual, or belief in the double existence of things—one existence in the sensible world, forever changing—another, inaccessible to direct observation, unchanging.

In the history of world views one cannot imagine that doctrinal variety will ever disappear in favor of a rigid monopoly by one system. This is why terms derived from the names of those who conceived original and far-reaching perspectives in philosophy, who formulated very widely accepted points of view, will surely survive. "Marxism" in this meaning of the term does not refer to a doctrine which can be either accepted as a whole or rejected as a whole. It does not mean a universal system but a vibrant philosophical inspiration, affecting our whole way of looking at the world; a stimulus forever active in the social intelligence and social memory of mankind. Its permanent validity is a consequence of the new and ever important perspectives which it opened to us: enabling us to look at human affairs through the prism of universal history; to see, on the one hand, how man in society is formed in the struggle against nature, and, on the other hand, the simultaneous process of humanizing nature by man's work; to consider thinking as a product of practical activity; to unmask myths of consciousness as being the result of ever-recurring alienations in social existence and to trace them back to their proper sources. These perspectives enable us, furthermore, to analyze social existence with its incessant conflicts and struggles. These conflicts and struggles, these countless multitudes of individual goals and desires, individual sufferings and disappointments, individual defeats and victories, present nonetheless a picture of a general evolution which—we have every right to believe—means, in the grand scale of history, not retrogression but progress.

Translated by George Krzywicki

Notes: 1950-1953

MAY 16, 1950

"Our task is to bring man closer to his most beautiful dreams, to his greatest hopes—to bring him closer to them in reality and in practice, so that Christians themselves can find the beginning of their heaven on this earth." (Garaudy)

As a figure of speech, this is quite good. But as a basis for a political party's program it is, I think, too much. Perhaps I underestimate the essence of the party, perhaps I minimize its tasks, its role and its objectives, but I believe that the lack of some such restriction opens the way for the Great Lie. Realization of the most beautiful dreams cannot be the objective of a political party, which is a machine of a special kind that can never reach the stars. This task will never be achieved by anyone, and it is better not to put it forth as a guiding aim —for it would end, not in the realization of heaven on earth, but in a communique from the Politburo stating that this heaven had already been achieved, in a popular holiday with parades and music in honor of the New Era. Let us build houses full of light; let us print wise books; let us hand the best traditions down to the workers; let us learn from them strength and endurance; let us create the socialist system— but let us not create the beginning of heaven on this earth, for it will end sadly.

OCTOBER 31, 1950

I think it is rather difficult for many revolutionaries to digest the conservative side of dialectics, which states that an economic-social system must exist until it fulfills its tasks— and that from the higher view of the history of dialectical progress it should exist until it does. Their psychology tends toward moralistic ahistoricism; in their evaluation of people belonging to the system against which they fight they are influenced by moral indignation. They look upon such people's motives as those of execrable puppets moved by the hands of vile forces. These psychological tendencies have no connection with theory; on the contrary, theory calls for almost superhuman objectivity, for concentrating on the inherent logic of things that accounts for human behavior, rather than on people's errors and crimes. The revolutionary's psychology is governed by the need to shift the responsibility for the whole weight of historical miseries onto some person. That is why it is so difficult to find in Marxist journalistic and literary works opinions which are up to the standards of the theory, which do not fall into an easy contempt or emotionalism, which are not characterized by the sort of horror stories created in the name of the grandeur of the Revolution. Russia already has discarded the horror stories—but only in relation to her own history. Moreover, in discarding them, Russia has been guided by motives and mental attitudes based on suspicion. This negation has been followed by organized adoration of the symbols of national glory, symbols irrelevant to the history of human progress. Thus *raison d'etat* is projected back into the past, and the classic words about the policeman of Europe, as applied to Suvorov[1] for instance, are no longer considered valid. The conservative side of dialectics has been adapted to a nationalistic hagiology.

NOVEMBER 11, 1950

"If you wish to create a Christian work of art, be a Christian, and search for a way to create a beautiful work of art proceeding from your heart; do not try to do it 'a la Christian.' If you convert esthetics into an article of faith, you spoil your faith. If you turn your devotion to God into a rule for artistic work, or your concern with edifying your fellowmen into a canon for your art, you spoil your art." (Maritain) Does not this perhaps also apply to the question of Socialist Realism? And is it worthwhile—so far as artists are concerned—to refer to Catholic theoreticians of art long preceding Maritain, who would not accept his opinion that "a Catholic work of art requires an artist to be free as an artist," and that "the artist's soul wholly reaches his work and directs it, but it should reach and direct it only through his artistic temperament." I think that it is not worthwhile. I believe that the "liberalism" of Marxists should be at least as liberal as that of the contemporary Father of the Church. . . .

MARCH 7, 1951

Marxism is a science of the *opportunities* for shaping man, but not of man himself. Marxism itself—within the limits of its beloved facts—requires interpretation, even a *personal* interpretation. . . .

SEPTEMBER 28, 1951

If, in a very narrow meaning of the word, all culture is to be at the service of the superstructure—if the writer is to

[1] Eighteenth century Russian general.

photograph the miner and the bricklayer, and thus not allow them any "transcendence," any trespassing of the limits of their everyday life in a direction other than the prescribed socialist future; if, for his part, the painter is to impress them with so many images of themselves that they cannot see anything in the world but their own heroic torsos in the leading role; if in the name of human happiness any kind of intellectualizing except that devoted to reversing the flow of rivers or transforming mountain chains is to be condemned to oblivion and regarded with contempt; if literature is to repeat the negative and positive of our times to infinity, i.e., capitalism as interpreted by writers in the school of critical realism, and socialism as interpreted by Stalin prize-winners; if human fate is to mean merely the road of social advancement or the exposure of the enemy; if the feeling of brotherhood is to be restricted to those who think in the same way; and if victory should unfortunately be won soon—then a pitiable fate would be in store for the System of the Great Engineer of Human Souls, the fate of a machine revolving in a vacuum. If the teachings of the Great Engineer were to exercise an irrevocable influence, if the object and the victim of that science—the New Man of the Socialist Epoch—were to lose all the condemned tendencies, he would die of despair on the threshold of that land of which humanity has been dreaming day and night, finding nothing with which to occupy his hands, no records to break, no peace to fight for. Or perhaps he would be forced to climb into an atomic airplane—already, incidentally, in the minds of the leading engineers—and conquer a new homeland a little retarded in its historical development, in which—fortunately—there would still be capitalism. Where is that Greece about which Marx, a forgotten idealist, had some vague notions? Or perhaps we ought to fight for the new and against the old now, when posters welcoming the Communist Epoch are being prepared in joyful after-work hours, when, in short, we are already at the point of embracing the ideal? Perhaps the "new" would mean a return to forbidden questions, to excommunicated feelings, to non-Leninist thoughts—to the fullness of individual development, about which something is written in the Manifesto? And perhaps we would find that everything of which we are so proud today is the "old"? Dialectics, the Queen of the World, can play practical jokes even on the Great Engineer who believes that not even she can surpass him; that, obedient to the commands of authority, she has transformed herself into tame criticism and self-criticism, and will do nothing without his instructions. But then the key of history, that fern flower[2] of all politicians and philosophers of history anxious to ride the steed of the Apocalypse to the ultimate Emancipation, would have to be in his pocket. Yet, I have an impression that it hovers over deep waters.

SEPTEMBER 28, 1951

On the Similarity of Contradictions

It is odd that the best guides to the mentality of our time are two books from different poles of the political landscape. Carl Schmidt's *Begriff des Politischen* is, in fact, a commentary on the Short Course.[3] Let none be offended, it is only a stratagem of the Objective Spirit, as Hegel would say. A stratagem in which the Objective Spirit employs, for its own aims, black and white, or rather black and red, good and evil, hot and cold. Both books are a manifestation of the spirit of Pure Politics, that fecund and deadly science of today. Pure Politics has come to occupy the throne vacated by Pure Economics, and we are now going through its classical period. Of what does its purity consist? It consists of this, that as in the past economics taught everyone the necessity of abiding by the principle of profit under penalty of elimination from the race of free competition, so now Pure Politics is pushing into oblivion every-

---

[2] A rare, mysterious flower, which according to legend blossoms on a midsummer night and brings good fortune. T.N.

[3] Official history of the Communist Party of the Soviet Union.

thing that is not compatible with the principle of political usefulness. All values must either submit or perish. The world becomes monistic, pure, politically pure. Everything yields to the power of this political purpose which is determined by committees of men of contemporary wisdom. They pronounce judgment on it with all the precision of blind intellect. They do not understand that the principle of Perfect Security will end in everyone's spying upon everyone else; they do not see that the principle of Absolute Mobilization will, having reached the breaking point, snap like a string on a bow. They do not understand that the principle of Incessant Enthusiasm leads to a sclerosis of the heart, and that the principle of dividing the world into Enemies and Friends often results in rejecting the kernel for the chaff. They do not remember that greed for power lies in wait for committees of wizards. Pure Politics will leave behind it a ravaged battlefield, torn shoots, blood-stained hopes—and an emptiness within the hearts of the disillusioned. . . .

SEPTEMBER 30, 1951

. . . An exceedingly oppressive influence was exerted on the socialist mind by an abnormally aggressive psychology which, suspecting Fascism everywhere, often surrendered wild and "uncertain" flowers to the adversary. Zolkiewski[4] surrendered even Mounier to Truman because Mounier did not agree with Zhdanov on the question of Tito. The whole period of the last fifty years was evaluated from these exceedingly narrow, mistrustful, psychologically abnormal and often backward positions, which resulted in a climate of belligerence within the movement and in intellectual laziness. Analysis was replaced by boastful philippics — the comprehension of manifold tendencies by sprinklings of holy water from the dogmatic jug. The movement was so impressed with its own omniscience, and became so conceited, that a vacuum began

---

[4] Leading Communist ideologist and official in Poland.

to form in its thinking. In fact, Russia was busy with her own tasks, and in Europe there was no capable man aside from Lukacs. It is already too late at the present stage to change, and a fantastic ignorance is being spread of that period. But for his Social Contract, even Rousseau might today be considered a forerunner of Fascism, because of his tartness toward the Encyclopedists and his cult of feeling and simplicity; obviously a fascist. Thus we are now returning to positions of scientism, rationalism, and similar respectabilities. As for man himself, we know nothing about him except that reality finds its reflection in him—sometimes in a right way, sometimes in a wrong way, sometimes in a reactionary or in a progressive way, but always reflected in man. In philosophy, we have not gone beyond empiro-criticism. We replace ethical analyses by tales of man as he should be. In brief, Europe is perishing, and are we victorious? Then why are we not rescuing Europe's treasures? Is it because we do not wish to see our own poverty?

OCTOBER 2, 1951

Objective Consequences of Paying Attention Only to Objective Consequences, or the Surprises of Dialectics

Somewhere in his writings Mannheim calls attention to the fact that the theory of conditioned reflexes, the Russian equivalent of behaviorism, underlies the actions of our apparatus of power, and that the pedagogy of mass propaganda consists, in fact, of eliciting associations and reflex actions without any special consideration for what all subjectivists call the "inner coverage." This should arouse great indignation on our part: was behaviorism not solemnly condemned as a filthy product of imperialism, as a system which looks upon people as machines for producing and killing, and overlooks their human dignity? Do we not stress the importance of a deep and sincere attitude to Party affairs and norms, and to the New Man's decalogue of virtues? Mannheim must be simply a slanderer, a lackey, a hired agent. But apparently this is not so. The mechanism of operation of a party of the Stalinist type, combined with the mechanist's theoretical dislike for all "subjectivism" (i.e., for taking notice of the undesirable inner experiences of people submitted to the machine's gears), leads in practice to the manufacture of conventionalized reflex actions which overwhelm man so completely as to suffocate in him all that cannot be expressed through them. Feelings not revealed in word, action, or impulse grow pale, like starving children. Thoughts which are not formulated lose their shape and pulse and become a flock of melancholy shadows.

In our time, the knowledge of how to extinguish all kinds of life other than that which has been planned is very desirable knowledge. This, however, could be said only by a nasty cynic; we say something different, namely, that the outward behavior of man is, or will be, an expression of his feelings. And so ardently and completely are we convinced of this thesis that we feel no need to prove it. Thus, day after day, incessantly and hopelessly, we write in our daily press: "They enthusiastically adopted ... they fervently approved the increase of norms ... they greeted with elation ... they held a rally, filled with anger." We ascribe to people planned, prescribed feelings on the basis of people's outward behavior interpreted according to our wishful thinking, and this goes on day after day, month after month; the question of the correspondence of feelings and reflex actions vanishes under the weight of convenience and in the haze of (political) obliviousness. In practice we cease to be concerned with it at all. In practice we are, so to say, retreating to the positions of behaviorism. The motives are allegedly different, but the objective consequences are identical. Yet, we were taught that objective consequences are the most important.

OCTOBER 5, 1951

Superstructure serves the base. This simple, supposedly very brilliant statement has behind it a whole philosophy of culture which, in my opinion, is not quite in agreement with that philosophy of freedom which had the proletariat of capitalism for its historical ally. Let us recall young Marx's conclusion on the indispensability of philosophy for the proletariat, and vice versa. It thus appears that sometimes, if only for purposes of contemplation, it is admissible to take a "detached" attitude, and to contemplate earthly matters from the lofty stand of that philosophy which once demanded only active realization. If we examine, from this point of view, the theory and practice of relations between the superstructure and the base in the happy countries of socialism, we shall come to some rather sad conclusions. This theory of subordination stems from the historical analysis of class systems, i.e., systems whose symbols, mass beliefs and current ideas were supposed to strengthen institutions based on oppression, authority based on violence, wealth based on the exploitation of servile labor. Within those systems the superstructure always helped the leading institutions of the given epoch to assert themselves, to augment their power and their glory.

That is what could be said about this question in general outline, by taking into consideration the social functions of the superstructure from the point of view either of rulers or of their opponents. Some people would say it with satisfaction, others with bitterness, but the meaning does not lie in these psychological trifles. The meaning is this, that both these groups project one aspect, purely political, onto the whole structure of cultural phenomena, and do not take notice of those parts which are the secret source of culture, a condition of its sustaining life, if life is to be expressed not merely in the supply of goods to landowners, municipalities, clergy, judiciary, and central committees. This theory is guilty of a certain emotional omission, one of many of which the revolutionary movement has been guilty, that yields to the "psychology of contrast" traced by Plekhanov in his studies of the development of literary genres. What this means is simply that the utilization of a certain value—be it a concept, a symbol, a theory, or an institution—by one of the battling groups or classes, results in almost automatic negative reactions on the other side of the barricade. This happened to the conception of nation, state, family, duty, honor, love, etc. *The way in which a certain value is being used overshadows its real meaning.* The theory of subordination has all the features of a theory constructed on the basis of such automatic reflex actions. Furthermore, as has been noticed by many people, both Marxists and laymen, it explains neither the phenomenon of permanence of the highest cultural values, nor the psychology of creativity. This, incidentally, also applies to the theory of the absolute class character of knowledge.

Does this theory, then, separated from class relations and availing itself—for its own purposes—of the political wisdom and technique of its century-long adversaries, operate to bring about a period when all traces of the class character of culture (together with the somewhat exaggerated concern with subordination of superstructure to the base) will vanish? I think not. At some time in the future, gratitude toward life will not be considered suspect because it is directed to nobody in particular. Sorrow and song will accompany the life of man, who will no longer find it necessary to worry lest the first deprive him of the optimism appropriate to those living in a Socialist State, or to be concerned that the second imitate the sound of the Peace Dove's flight. This will, of course, come at some future date, not today. But perhaps it would be worthwhile to prepare the holy paths—the thoughts which, presumably, will be needed, and which will become a superstructure of the new period, the period to be brought about if the epoch of the State Monopoly of Culture does not last forever.

OCTOBER 12, 1951

The Knowledge Possessed by the "Engineers of Souls"

The knowledge of human souls which is at the disposal of the Engineers of our time is astonishingly insignificant. That is why in practice we have recourse rather to the massive and safe rules of magic than to the commonplace slogans which are fit only for posters. In the first phase of the revolution it was still said that matters concerning man would not be taken up until after a period of fifty years. Today, a similar approach to this question would be considered an offense. Is not the new man already here? It is he who survived the Battle of Stalingrad, he who went on to conquer Berlin, he who is planting new forests and reversing the flow of rivers. Let us bow our heads to this "authentic man," for he is the symbol of all those who held firm during the patriotic war. But let us not think that this answers the question. That which is now so persistently recommended to us as a product of socialism is something so very simple and ancient that we cannot possibly see anything new in it. How can we pay homage to ourselves? As for the reversal of rivers—the epoch of the transformation of nature—we are well-satisfied with it. Our generation likes gigantic works; they give us vast glimpses of the transformation of life, and show us the style of our time. Yet, is all this sufficient for us? I think not. Nowa Huta[5] does not prevent us from looking forward to the Glorious New World.

It would be difficult, indeed, not to use this latter symbol in referring to the knowledge of the Engineers. For we are now creating an absolute superstructure, eliminating from the world of culture, as one eliminates the plague, everything that might create in people a force not at the control of our magic. This force grows in the individual as a result of his efforts to acquire an independent attitude toward the most important values. That is why we do not awaken people, but teach them only catechisms. That is why we can permit growth only when we supervise it, with scissors in hand. That is why we exercise control over every inspirational gesture of man, over everything that is an independent attempt to reach for the values of art, religion, and morality. For our knowledge does not

---

[5] An industrial development built by the Communists outside Cracow.

include these phenomena, our magic feels itself endangered, and our practice, based on magic, is losing its efficacy. Thus we spread over people and the world the opaque dome of our superstructure. There are no stars but those we permit to shine. There are no experiences but those we allow the people to have.

And all the while, the jugglers of dialectical materialism are busy painting a sun on the vault and asking us to believe that no other sun exists.

OCTOBER 15, 1951

Has anything changed since that time when, in the abyss of night, uncertain of when it would end, we shrugged our shoulders at the assertions of determinists who maintained that socialism will win of necessity? It seemed to us then that their allegedly scientific assertions, their too-ready belief in their own dreams, implied some fear, some uncertainty, some inadequacy of attitude toward history, toward everything that cannot be foreseen in it. He who is not brave enough to face the unknown, who must have, if he wants to enter the future, a written guarantee of success, is not worthy of man's fate.

During the war we regarded the major part of socialist literature as such a guarantee. Our feelings certainly did not come from approving the world's tragedy, but from comparing those calculations with our experiences.

The present time does not entitle us to discard this basically distrustful attitude toward all deterministic beliefs. For this reason, the technicians of power do not incite our enthusiasm, and their lofty certitude makes us uneasy.

We are coming out to meet these values whose truth we discovered at the end of the night; we wish to be faithful to them whether the world accepts them as true or not. . . .

DECEMBER 1, 1951

Warnings of a Personalist

"Organization means progress toward order, but it can be carried only to a certain point, beyond which man is reduced to the dimension of his function. Socialization may be considered an achievement of the spiritual life, but it can take place only if personal initiative is not stifled by great mechanisms, and the boldness of intellect is not suppressed by conformism. Work, the participation in public and political life, creates a desirable balance to the danger of egocentric isolation and subjectivistic shapelessness. However, it may also become an instrument of dehumanization if it tries to abase and eliminate from life all that is represented by and results from reflection, silence, repose, inner drama, metaphysical disquietude, effort toward spiritual discipline, protest of conscience, and from the perpetual urge to humanize the social order and to imbue truth with personal meaning." (Emmanuel Mounier)

Participation in political and public life may become an instrument of dehumanization. It is this fragment of contemporary dialectics that the engineers of human souls failed to notice—or noticed only with applause.

DECEMBER 8, 1951

Regardless of the indignation of the high priests of dialectics, Bergson is right—at least in relation to us. Our intellect, our knowledge is, in fact, a knowledge of the sphere of things useful to our activities. That which lies beyond the horizon of our Party visibility is simply ignored. Of things with which we ourselves are not acquainted we most often learn from masks worn by our adversaries—and for this reason certain cultural values appear to us to be only masks, screening the diabolical face of enemy or non-believer. That is why our humanistic knowledge is so pitifully poor, except when treated as a part of social-economic history. We become utterly incapable of grasping values of life other than those which are useful from our specific, Party-derived point of view. We are a great factory producing xenophobia. We are partly saved by tradition which, incidentally, we hold in great esteem only because it was a steppingstone to perfecting ourselves. We are partly saved by the struggle for peace which permits us to indulge in the luxury of amiability toward those who think differently, and which even inclines us to be quite satisfied with ourselves as Europeans, able to experience feelings of such an exquisite kind. This margin for the approved "something other," however, also stems from our activities, and only from our activities, and it is defined by the line of our propaganda. Beyond this there is a wilderness and a land of enmity. There we store everything which does not fit into the sphere of things useful to the building of our superstructure. For this reason, the prevailing consciousness of our time is the consciousness of the *political controller of life*. Here lies the source of our attitude toward spontaneity, the partial recognition of which would cast a shadow upon the controller's omnipotence. . . .

MARCH 8, 1952

The Critical Consciousness and the Dogmatic Consciousness or About Things Which Are Seldom Spoken of in Poland

"The critical consciousness knows that the world in which it exists is full of problems, that it is a questionable, unfinished world where creative and never completed human activity leaves its traces. The dogmatic consciousness cuts itself off from the risk and the uncertainty of changing reality, and strives toward a world which is systematically deprived of problems, a world in which questions are replaced by puffed-up axioms. Such a world liberates man from the burden of freedom, a freedom which imposes upon him the hard task of continually renewing, not only the essence of concepts which order his knowledge of the world, but also their form, the very categories of perception. When applying these considerations to Marxism, we are faced with a peculiar antinomy inherent in the core of the intellectual culture of the Marxist movement. Marxism puts a particular stress on the criticism of all kinds of mythologies, on achieving a transition from utopian to scientific socialism, from a system of metaphysics of eternal truths to historical recognition of the relative and problematic character of truths of a given period. At the same time, however, by becoming a kind of popular faith, similar to the old faiths which cling to the Apocalypse and the advent of the Millennium, by augmenting its strength through the assimilation of the powerful energies of popular religious beliefs, Marxism has also absorbed certain elements which are extremely dangerous to the free development of the movement itself, and to the searching mind. This, of course, must not be exaggerated. The history of culture knows many examples of this kind of antinomy. Nevertheless, it is a fact that should be recognized and described, a question that should be taken up by Marxists with the utmost seriousness and clarity, if we are not to surrender it to the enemy who will come forth with it as a defender of freedom and culture, thus converting the whole problem into a political slogan." (Remo Cantoni: "Elements of Myth and Criticism in Marxist Culture," *Esprit*, May 1948.)

In this manner, Cantoni states the existence of tension between popular and scientific culture, between culture and policy *within the movement*. The requirements imposed upon culture by policy do not always serve the cause of socialist culture. Critical thinking does not always answer the needs of masses engaged in the struggle, nor is it always to the liking of the revolutionary headquarters, accustomed to receiving obedience. It is not worthwhile to veil this fact by accusing thinkers of the tendency to withdraw to an ivory tower, of elitism, or of Trotskyism. The inconclusiveness that would result from the consideration of these matters, or the recognition of these tensions, leads us to put culture at the service of Party policy, and science at the service of mythology, with a light-heartedness characteristic of our Party. We are building a perfectly obedient world, a world without conflicts, a world governed by circulars of the Omnipotent Departments, a world without blemish from the standpoint of effective governing, but not exempt from fear on the part of its victims, and all those for whom the omnipotence of the apparatus means the peril of socialist culture.

MARCH 14, 1952

We look on the past as if each of the various cultures had its central committee which, with a perfection equal to ours, mastered the remunerative art of building a *useful* superstructure. There is, of course, some exaggeration in this statement, but it describes a limit toward which our interpretations of past ideological struggles tend; the more tenaciously so, the greater the influence of those cultures and the greater their role in influencing public opinion. There are many examples of this. Our statements come back to us as recurrent echoes, and we ascribe mystical meaning to them, call them the voice of the class, bow to them, and—seriously and semi-consciously playing a comedy of obedience to ourselves—proclaim obedience to the class instinct. In our country, Marxist knowledge of ideologies has already penetrated the thatched roofs (Mickiewicz's phrase for the masses—T.N.), but in a shape given to it by people so accustomed to manipulation in the cultural field that they now believe everything which came before them also to have been the result of manipulation. Our theory, which yields to the social demands of this cadre of activists, seems to forget that there were times when culture was also an expression of experiences, not only of interest, of perceptions, not only of instructions, of feelings, not only of calculations. This is one trend in the not unintentional distortion of our theory of culture. The second trend consists of this, that every value which lies as an obstacle on the road to our political goals we define also as "political," thus—by means of this simple device—clearing away all moral norms which might rise higher than the principle of political usefulness. A relative truth becomes here an unconditional absolution of conscience. . . .

MARCH 23, 1952

On the Impossibility of Applying Cartesian Method in the Teaching of Marxism

"I must never accept anything as true until I perceive it as such, i.e., I must avoid hurry and prejudice and must not include in my judgment anything except that which will rise before my intellect so clearly and distinctly that it will be impossible to question it." (Descartes: *Discourse on Method*.)

Unfortunately, this first principle of the Cartesian method, which is simply a rule for good work, cannot be applied today on a more significant social scale. We avoid the possibility of doubt not by methods indicated by the author of the treatise on the passions of the soul, but by an entirely different method, namely by arousing these passions against those who question us. In a period of transition everything is excusable, but we are now losing even the guarantee of renovation—the sense that something is not in order in this world which allegedly is soon to become the best of worlds. Briefly, we are losing the sense of decency. With one hand we place Descartes' monument in the Pantheon of Progress, and with the other we threaten those who show a tendency to follow his instructions. . . .

MAY 25, 1952

On the Dialectics of Marxism

"In its further development, materialism becomes one-sided. Knowledge based on the senses loses its poetical blossom, it passes into the abstract experience of the mathematician; geometry is proclaimed as the queen of sciences. Materialism takes to misanthropy. If it is to overcome its opponent, misanthropic, fleshless spiritualism, and that on the latter's own ground, materialism has to chastise its own flesh and become ascetic." (Marx on English Materialism, *Selected Works*, Volume I, pp. 406-7.)[6]

Thus, it appears that in the course of history there have been periods when materialism became misanthropic; when, through its abstract, geometrical character, it became alienated from knowledge based on the senses; when it chastised the flesh and became ascetic in order to meet the requirements of the battle against its opponent. It appears that at times the logic of battle may be viewed from a point beyond the historical point of view, so that we pass judgment on the harmfulness both of enemies and avowed friends. My impression is that unfortunately our materialism, which builds a system equal in beauty to the Palace of Culture, clad in the armor of ruthless struggle against idealism, is slowly turning hostile to man, like the materialism of those other times; that the aroma of human life other than that which pervades the voluntary labor camps, exemplary schools, academy meetings, banquets of leading workers and military manoeuvres, is slowly deserting the land. We are a generation brought up in squads, occupation teams, youth organizations, with rifles in our knapsacks so as not to be suspected of individualism. But the aroma of human life cannot be limited to the repertoire of these institutions. We have become ascetics of the geometry of organized life.

JUNE 12, 1952

. . . It seems that we are organically incapable of taking into account that which is *unexpected*. We think that we have already tamed dialectics to such a degree that it will

---

[6] In the English edition, these considerations are ascribed to Engels and appear in the chapter: Engels on Historical Materialism—T.N.

never grow above our heads, that we shall never be frightened at the sight of tares coming up with the wheat we sowed. We think that we have absorbed all contradictions so that none of them will ever come forth against us. We give this optimism as spiritual nourishment to our generation, and let it helplessly face the experiences of time. Any kind of warning we take as a manifestation of weakness, an enemy instigation, an adversary's stratagem. With this frail perspective we bind our whole faith, strength, and consciousness. That is why we fail to notice the issues which are potentially dangerous.

Thus, we witness here the reappearance of a rather tenacious historical phenomenon, namely that those engaged in some activity are not fully aware of the consequences of their actions, so that eventually these are taken into account by some opponent. This is proved by many examples. We are fully and systematically unaware of that which can be defined as *political alienation*, and which consists of the fact that the State has raised itself high above the masses. We bathe—at any rate in books and in the press—in the illusion of almost complete democracy. We reprint Marx's and Lenin's articles on the Commune as though our officials were also elected, and their highest salary did not exceed the wages of a worker. We refrain from criticizing these illusions so as not to reveal too many of the peculiarities of our power apparatus which recognizes as hostile even the theory of the "equality of stomachs." We write that the Party does not create privileges but only duties—and we do not at all analyze the activities of the personnel offices with which every non-Party man comes into contact and from which he makes this analysis for us.

We do not wish to listen to the voices of those who stand outside the current and who thus are better able to see the foam and ferment of the *unexpected*. We cut ourselves off from the world dialogue, from the remarks of strangers and friends, by the stigmata of hostility with which we mark every sentence that has the misfortune not to be to our liking. Despite the lessons of history, we think we are perfectly able to comprehend all our doings with our own eyes. That is why, instead of absorbing, we reject any criticism that is unacceptable to us, criticism which is independent of us and which must accumulate beside us, and against us, because it is more and more difficult for us to discard illusions. We are ear-deep in the world of Hegelian, niggling reason, which, unaware of anything without, puffs itself up, only to fall finally into the mad belief of its own exclusiveness.

JUNE 13, 1952

On the Confrontation of Perspectives and on the Spirit of the Times Speaking in Different Languages

The spirit of our times speaks in a language similar to that of the Communist Manifesto, and without bothering to notice the fact that Stalin orders it to adhere to Schelling's metaphysics and observe things as immobile and abstract. "Economic conflicts come within the orbit of the most essential matters concerning human fate," states Z. Kubiak in *Przeglad Powszechny*. Marxism, like the Holy Ghost, hovers today over vast waters. We seem not to notice it, and—as a rule—we do not try to confront the perspectives. We are conceited and negligent like all who come to believe in their own monopoly of truth. Nobody knows why we still call ourselves dialecticians, and when it was we lost the graceful art of dialogue. We repeat over and over again: "Existence defines thought," not seeing that the core of this truth has already pervaded all the leading trends. Today, if it is still worthwhile to engage in dialogue, it should certainly not be carried on with outsiders—of whom we are so very fond—but with those who recognize this core and who combine this recognition with their knowledge of cultures different from ours.

Only this can enable the development of a Marxism which is something different from a succession of celebrations in honor of Joseph the Patriarch.

JUNE 22, 1952

On Civil Laws Contradictory to the Law of Nature, or the Fourth Chapter of Book 26, Volume II

"Gondebaud, the king of Burgundy, decreed that if the wife or the son of a thief did not reveal his crime, they should be deprived of their personal freedom. This law was in contradiction to nature. How is it possible for a wife to be the accuser of her husband? How can a son be the accuser of his father? In order to punish a crime, the law required the committing of another, still more criminal act."

We do not issue such laws. For us, the command of Party conscience is sufficient. Nor do we at all agree with Montesquieu's commentary. The spirit of our laws is different. We destroy the narrower solidarities if they are opposed to the rationale of the central, supervisory organ. In our opinion the analogy between us and Gondebaud is only apparent, because his law was at the service of the interests of the mighty, whereas our conscience protects the property of our society, our Party, and our class. We look upon Montesquieu as a liberal who desired to keep the State from interfering in the sacred bourgeois domain—the sphere of private life. We reject the sacred character of that sphere. We subordinate nature to the Party.

SEPTEMBER 6, 1952

On Perpetual Discussion as a Specific Aspect of Our System

(On the occasion of the All-Polish Conference of the National Front)

In our country, the word "discussion" has a specific meaning. One can analyze political systems as one does instruments of production. Thus feudalism can be compared to a water mill and capitalism to a steam mill, as was done by the young Marx who, like all young men, had a tendency toward intellectual bravado. But in analyzing these things we can employ not only economics but semantics as well. It may seem that this is a purely idealistic method. Yet I shall try to prove that this is not so, and that the analysis of the present meaning of the word "discussion" will show us the actual relations between people and organizations in our transitory system. Paraphrasing Marx, it could be said that "discussion," in the meaning given to it in the past, represents capitalism, and in the present meaning, socialism. Therefore, let us examine the way in which our discussions reveal the specific problems of socialism.

First: the rite which we call discussion reveals the heartfelt unity of conviction among all who participate in it. In a capitalist society, torn by contradictions, discussion is carried on by several parties and from several different vantage points. In our system this is not necessary at all, because under our system there are only two categories of people: those who want socialism, and those who do not want it. The first category is strong, coherent, ready for action, without any inclination to split hairs. The second category of people is generally not included in discussion, or, if it is, the discussion does not take place in public. In this way we consolidate ourselves, raise our spirits, speak among ourselves of how bad it was in the past, write our own biographies, praise our leaders, promise to double our efforts—and all this, all this solemn talk, we call discussion. The other side is also represented in these discussions, but not personally. It is introduced by the ministrant of the rite at the outset of the discussion, in the shape of information as to the opinions and plans entertained by enemies of national unity; this throws the whole audience into a frenzy of maledictions and accusations, and leads to mutual warnings and appeals for vigorous counteraction.

We are continually engaged in this kind of discussion, submerging ourselves alternately in the depths of holy enthusiasm and of holy indignation, filling our Sundays and holidays which, under the capitalist system, were spent in contemplative solitude according to the customs of bourgeois individualism.

Second: Our discussions reveal a complete harmony between the Party leadership and the whole society. They never move along lines unknown to our leadership; they are held at times and places foreseen by the plan. Previously, such harmony was an unattainable ideal for any society, but today the ideal has been brought down to earth, as Norwid dreamt.

Third: These rites give evidence of the masses' deep reverence for their benefactors—the Leaders of the People's State who provide these masses with entertainment, clothing, weapons, employment, schools for their children, and send their enemies to the place of eternal rest. This reverence which overflows people's hearts demands to be expressed, and that is why the warm milk of blessing so often pours upon the heads of our authorities, fostering the rite of Perpetual Discussion, the basic custom of this Most Perfect of Democracies.

SEPTEMBER 12, 1952

Historicity—The Ideology of Those Who Do Not Like Comparisons

Nothing is truer than our beloved statement that cultures, systems, and formations represent certain wholes whose parts are closely connected with and mutually dependent on one another, shaped by their role in the system of mutual correlations. The monopoly of political power, state economy, theocracy in the Zulu country or Cambodia—all these are different from our sacred institutions. We keep repeating with much ado the well-known truth about complete unanimity, and we imagine ourselves to be the leaders of the world. In consequence we are losing knowledge of the real qualities of our thinking—of our real similarities to, and differences from, the rest of polluted humanity. This remainder of humanity has for long been imbued with the conviction that the world is changeable, and it does not at all believe in the everlasting existence of capitalism, in the unchangeability of virtues, in

197

the static character of values. Even the theologians want to learn from Marx the ways of teaching Church History and—convinced in their own way—they proclaim the weakness of spirit when confronted with the pressure of matter, illustrating it with examples taken from the holiest Scriptures. Today the world looks upon its past in a different way than at the time the Manifesto appeared. Marxism has already accomplished its task—it has permeated the whole of culture. It has destroyed the reign of the much-esteemed Absolutes; it has imbued the patricians with a spirit of regard for the plebs; it has put down the mighty from their seats and exalted those of low degree. It seems, however, that it has succumbed to the fate which is ascribed by Hegel to all concrete manifestations of spirit. It has become a *prisoner of its own (ingenious) ideas*. It began by serving them; it has fallen under their yoke.

So far as words are concerned, Marxism is still creative—but in some matters it has become an ideology totally subservient to acts against its spirit. The historical basis of law is one of the principles in regard to which we now begin to reveal not-quite-pure feelings, feelings tinged with disquiet, appearing in the guise of holy indignation. We refuse to realize that there exist certain laws of structure which embrace all creations in the *great domains of spirit and of violence*. On the grounds of their very definition, these laws presumably contradict the historical principle of law—as if it were not true that various structural laws can function within the framework of various entities. The thesis on the historical basis of law which instructs us to reject *a priori* all such considerations, has changed from a scientific rule into an ideology of people who do not like comparisons.

SEPTEMBER 27, 1952

Conversation with J.

J. said that the position from which it is most difficult to achieve the transition to Communism is socialist idealism, the idealism of good people of the imperialist period, intellectuals who broke with the bourgeois system in search of the Holy Trinity of laymen: Goodness, Beauty, and Truth; workers dreaming about the splendor of the classless system; girls longing for a world governed by the tenderness and the mutual help of guiltless and beautiful people. This is the position from which it is most difficult to meet that reality which is far harder and darker than dreams and appearances. Reaching into his own experience, he also said that a much better point of departure is afforded by Catholicism, hierarchical Catholicism devoid of dreams about the good man, preaching the burden of earthly life and the remoteness of heaven.

OCTOBER 5, 1952

On the Tragedy of Deferring to Infinity

"Only after it disarms the bourgeoisie, will the proletariat—without disclosing its historical task—be able to throw on the garbage heap *all its weapons*; this it will certainly do, but on no account sooner than at that time." (Lenin: "On the Slogan of Disarmament," page 229.)

We plan to fulfill all the items included in the bourgeois concert of desires; we are faithful to the eighteenth century's super-program—only we never think of doing it right away, and are always putting it off for a little while, to some later date. We would be willing to throw on the garbage heap all the nasty things which shock the sensitive spirit of the enlightened philosopher dreaming of a world without feudal fear, noise of weapons, and bloodshed. We would gladly throw into the garbage the state, the army, armaments, and all other horrible things which torment the liberal's heart. In our theoretical dislike for these apparatuses we are the truest of liberals, repeating the inspired prayers of the leading visionaries of the liberal religious denomination from the Abbé de Saint-Pierre to Wilhelm Foerster. Only, under the pressure of dialectics, we cannot give in yet. Dreams will be realized on this earth at the time of relaxation, after the death of the last enemy. Liberalism is one of these enemies; it prevents us from developing full fighting efficiency and postpones the time when we shall achieve our most noble liberal ideals. That is how the matter looks in Marxist theory. . . .

OCTOBER 28, 1952

Rosa Luxemburg on the Laws of Our Development

"In all public institutions without unrestricted freedom of press and association, without free exchange of opinion, life declines, becomes merely an appearance of life in which bureaucracy is the only active element. This is a law to which there are no exceptions." (La Revolution Russe, French re-edition, 1945, page 27.)

The operation of that law, i.e., the process of the displacement of life by appearances, is a carefully hidden ailment of our system. We support, as well as we can, the shaken monuments of the old democratic virtues bearing the traditional names of Discussion or Freedom of Elections, in order to make it difficult for people to understand the fact that freedom in our country is merely a well-understood necessity. We organize discussion, and exclude our opponents from them. Our new revolutionary order very willingly employs the old conservative technique of power, and proudly proclaims that its class content glorifies its application and excludes all comparisons. The result, however, is similar because this is a law from which there are no exceptions. It is a pity that we do not care to see it.

Unrestricted freedom of the press and association is not possible at a time of revolution. Yet, are we really doing everything possible to prevent the Party bureaucracy from becoming the only living element? Or, perhaps, we do not care about it? If so, this is because it is easier to govern the apparent life than the true one. We give the name "life" to the mere appearance of it, so that we may enjoy the sense of controlling the elements.

OCTOBER 30, 1952

About the Longing for the Universalism of Science

Generally, we are not acquainted with higher levels of the new, contemporary "German ideology," the ideology of the predecessors and the leading intellectual luminaries of Hitler's period. For this reason it seems to us that we are quite unique in our irreconcilable criticism of bourgeois science; not suspecting the bad neighborhood, we are naive and carefree. It seems to us that we are the only ones who set purifying fire to the edifice of the universalism of science, seat of the great spiritual plague which is called, in turn, cosmopolitanism and objectivism. In our opinion, this edifice—like everything else against which we choose to fight—is an abode of Fascists. This shows how illusory, tactical, dialectical, and alien to us is our defense of all values of bourgeois science against rightist attacks. Raising banners has become with us a tactical manoeuvre, a cool strategic regulation alien to the spontaneity of revolutionary passion. We do not consider it our duty to worship the slogans which we uphold. Yet, the defenders of those slogans have a duty to worship us. Should they, carried away by enthusiasm, be imprudent enough to put fidelity to slogans before fidelity to the dialectical followers of these slogans, then they become our enemies.

Objectivity of science—it seems that we have never understood the heartfelt esteem and reverent devotion to all social and intellectual values which were symbolized by this concept at the time of our disdain and the sharpening of Hitlerite knives. The concept of the objectivity of science was not meant to be a pretext for a desire to escape from participation in history, from brotherhood in arms, from the administering of justice to the perishing world. It was not the proverbial washing of one's hands of the matter, withdrawing to a safe and soothing land of pure science, from where it would be possible to look upon the struggling world as from behind a heavenly curtain. It was not a school of lofty neutrality—it was a school of battle. It was a time when even love was learn-ing to shoot, when the concept of evil acquired again its old impact of fear, its absolute dimension. Objectivity of science found itself in the front line of struggle against the diabolic invasion. It appeared that—in spite of numerous appearances and games of cynicism—it had hot blood and that it was in itself a measure of values.

We behave as if we did not want to know anything about it. There is method to this ignorance.

NOVEMBER 4, 1952

On the Revenge of Conventionalism

Our sociology of science has become a kind of technique for eliciting conditioned reflexes. The word "bourgeois" takes the place of a bell which elicits, with repulsion, the anticipated reaction of saliva flooding the mouth. Our aim is that every thought which has not been entered in the catalogue and pro-vided with the seal of Party censorship should automatically produce a hostile reflex action. Philosophy composed in sup-port of this technique of struggle for absolute power over human souls tries to reduce each manifestation of individual creativity, each thought, each stroke of the painter's brush to the role of a class excrement. Our fear of idealism reaches the limit beyond which caution changes into the absurd. We justly fight against those who see in the struggle of ideas only a dialogue of humanists, and are unable to see in it even a trace of class struggle. By the same token we, in turn, are reluctant to see in the struggle of ideas elements which go beyond the struggle of the two camps. This revenge taken on high-minded spirits exercises a rather disagreeable influence upon our humanistic science, art, and culture, because it en-titles us to introduce into these fields the methods flourishing in the arena of political struggle. From that moment, the sentence of the Politburo becomes the court of last appeal. Thus, our philosophical system reveals a tendency to transform itself into a deductive system inferring the criterion of truth from conformity with political axioms. This is the great revenge of conventionalism.

On Exercising Control Over Men and Objects or on the Utopian Heritage in Marxism

The old, allegedly socialist idea of controlling *objects* rather than *men* is based on a thoroughly bourgeois assumption. The *Ancien Régime* did not control objects; production and circulation of *objects* was in the hands of the bourgeoisie; hence the easiness, belligerence and pathos of this opposition; hence the bright hopes and illusions. Control over men was based on compulsion, control over *objects* on free association and free contract. Control over men stemmed from the inequality of various social strata, from the desire to maintain the old privileges; control over objects required the abolition of social strata, the introduction of equality under the law, the abolition of privileges harmful to healthy exchange. This opposition was a vehicle of bourgeois hopes, the instrument of bourgeois struggle, and the essence of the bourgeois utopia. Let us see what has happened since.

Utopian socialism inherited this opposition, thus putting off the day of realization to a later period yet to come. Scientific socialism enthusiastically acknowledged its relationship to utopian socialism, pending only the discovery of a rational, infallible key to this sesame of happy anarchy. Even Lenin wanted to simplify the system of controlling industry as he still believed in the possibility of almost immediate people's rule.

Yet, it somehow happens that the more we control objects, the stronger becomes our control over men. Utopia grows more and more distant. Recently it has withdrawn to the epoch of world economy, to the world without wars or states, without economic differences between various parts of the earth. Now the socialist utopia stubbornly adheres to an economic model which is more like a cooperative laundry than a world combine, in which the transparency of the administration's activities is supposed to be almost as clear to all interested persons as is the balance sheet of the laundry at the Warsaw Housing Cooperative to its membership of housewives. We take advantage of the old bourgeois utopias in order to convert them into myths that mask the great scissor blades of hope and reality. Thanks to this, we do not have to disturb our superstructure which tries to mask a reality similar, not to the old utopia, but to a modernized fairy tale—a fairy tale about a sorcerer's apprentice.

MAY 25, 1953

About the Forgotten Cathedrals

We celebrate, as thankful heirs, the memory of the eighteenth century, perceiving its bourgeois limitations only in the fact that it could not fulfill its promises. We appropriate its heritage, providing it only with better political techniques and with the friendship of the more faithful classes. We take over many of its most magnificent impulses—which is to our credit. At the same time, however, we take over many of its importunities, buffooneries, presumptions—which brings us into disrepute. We do not wish to remember that it was a century that did not understand Shakespeare, that shrugged its shoulders at the Gothic cathedrals which it wanted to sweep off the landscape together with feudal castles. We do not care to remember that in order to defend the place in history of Shakespeare and the cathedrals it was necessary to fight *against* the spirit of the times, that without the cultural results of the romantic reaction it would be impossible to imagine the politically neutral and relatively universal conviction as to traditional cultural values that we have today.

Even this single example should be a matter of reflection for the present ministers of culture and for all those who think that our superstructure contains in itself, as did sesame, all the treasures of the world, that the future will be born only from it, without the resurrection of values to which we are blind today.

Will we really have the future eating only from our hands? Do we really believe that we shall be able to tame the men of the future to such a degree that they will become oblivious to those cathedrals which we condemn to obscurity and contempt? Will no rejected beauty claim worship for itself—and forgiveness for us? If this be so, history will cease to be dialectical. Although we think that we have fully succeeded in making dialectics the servant of our *raison d'etat*, the Spirit of the World laughs aloud at such presumption. And for those who will come after us it is preparing a concert to be played on the strings of cathedrals which we—allegedly in the name of progress and revolution—chose to ignore.

Translated by Jadwiga Wojciechowska

About the Authors

TADEUSZ ROZEWICZ is perhaps the most original and talented of Poland's postwar poets, and one of the most representative voices in modern Polish writing. Now in his thirties, he published his first volumes of poetry soon after the Communists took power and was immediately criticized for his obsessive preoccupation with war — its cruelty and onslaught against human dignity. Unable to find a place for himself in the confusing reality of Polish life, he consciously limited his focus to the gloomier aspects of human existence and reproached man for his escape from responsibility and self-wisdom. In the past few years, Rozewicz has begun to take a more active part in contemporary reality, and not long ago the State awarded him a prize for his long poem, *The Plains*, in recognition of his creative achievements. The piece included here, which was originally published in the February 1957 issue of *Tworczosc* (Warsaw), conveys the poet's search for positive values in an atmosphere filled with the echoes of war's negation.

KAZIMIERZ BRANDYS began his literary career shortly before the last war. A Communist and indeed a leftist almost by temperament, he took seriously the Marxist view of the writer's role in society, and wrote much and incessantly throughout the postwar period, trying his hand at both the novel and the short story, with best results in the latter. After producing a number of more or less successful novels, for which he was awarded a State prize, he went through a stage of "socialist realism"; despite present trends, he has never disclaimed responsibility for this phase of his writing. His most recent and best-known works, *The Roman Hotel*, *The Defense of Granada* and *The Mother of Krole* (the title is a play on words; *krol*, used here as a surname, means *king* in Polish) have been widely praised for their sincere — if not always clear — analyses of past errors and abuses. Much of Brandys' work seems to be inspired by his dual role as intellectual and Communist. This "double vision" has sometimes led him into ambiguity, but through it he has produced some of the most perceptive and adventurous writing in present-day Poland. *The Defense of Granada*, which suggests some of the author's underlying conflicts, was first published in *Tworczosc*, January 1956.

A relative newcomer, ZBIGNIEW HERBERT published his first book of poems (*A Chord of Light*) in 1956, and was immediately accepted as an important younger poet. He is predominantly a philosophical poet, but this applies only to his choice of subject matter; technically, he is a lyricist with a strong feeling for the physical world. He does not hesitate to deal with the grand themes of truth and chaos, or reality and illusion, but he always uses concrete personalized words and images. Neither affirmative nor rebellious (in this, he is unlike Rozewicz), Herbert seems to be writing apart from the main stream of Polish life, using only those of its phenomena which come into direct contact with his vision. This attitude is not uncommon among his contemporaries. It has been called a form of escapism through verbal structure from the prosaic content of everyday life. Herbert has created a world of his own values and in *The Philosophers' Den* has used them to approach contemporary reality by a circuitous route through antiquity. The play was first published in *Tworczosc*, September 1957.

Although he began his career as a poet, WIKTOR WOROSZYLSKI is primarily a political writer — fiery, courageous and intellectually honest. Though minor, his poems are not without significance. Written under the influence of Mayakovsky, they nevertheless retain an original character: their tone is well-suited to Poland's milder "revolutionary" climate, and he manages to catch the true spirit of Polish radicalism. Throughout his work, he has shown a great readiness to examine and reexamine his conscience as it reacts to each phase of political life. As his "Notes" explain, he was one of the writers sent to observe the Soviet Union at first hand, and it was here that he went through a crisis of revolutionary faith. Upon his return to Poland, he played a prominent part in setting the intellectual stage for the Polish October, did some reporting (notably on the Poznan riots) and allied himself with the liberalizing forces. Given Woroszylski's particular temperament, it seems likely that he will continue to work for the ideals of his youth so long as he sees at least some reflection of them in reality. The Polish government's often ambiguous stand on culture, however, has already caused some conflict between him and his faith. The selection of his work included here was published in *Nowa Kultura* (Warsaw), March 25, 1956.

PAWEL HERTZ — like his more famous colleague, poet Adam Wazyk — has always been deeply interested in, and therefore considerably influenced by, Western culture, especially that of France. Classical in form and content, his poetry often strikes a gloomy note, but never reaches utter pessimism. Hertz spent the war years as a prisoner in Russia, and this experience seems to have strengthened his conviction that man is alone and that, precisely because of this, he must seek contact with others. It is said that his stay in Russia awakened his interest in Russian literature (Hertz subsequently translated many Russian books), but it is also possible that the insistence throughout the Stalinist period that everything Russian was great, influenced his course of activities. After 1953, Hertz gradually came to be regarded as one of the prominent, although not too prolific, spokesmen for liberalism within the Communist Party. Recently, after an unsuccessful attempt to start a Polish periodical *(Europa)* dedicated to Western art and culture, Hertz resigned as one of the magazine's editors and handed in his Party card in protest against the government's interference in the editorial policies of periodicals and newspapers. His essay "Recollections from the House of the Dead" first appeared in *Przeglad Kulturalny* (Warsaw), October 18, 1956.

Now in his thirties, LESZEK KOLAKOWSKI for a long time appeared to accept the orthodox Stalinist line in philosophy, and devoted most of his energies to attacks on Neo-Thomism and American pragmatism. After 1953, however, he gradually became the chief philosophical spokesman for what is now called "revisionism." Recently, his writings have come under strong attack by Stalinists everywhere, particularly in the Soviet Union, and it has been charged that by his present attempts to redefine Marxism he is departing from Marxism altogether. In the West, he is known chiefly for his satirical essay, "What Socialism Is Not," and for a series of articles entitled "History and Responsibility," which are aimed at a rejection of "moral historicism" — i.e., the theory which maintains that history provides the ultimate criterion of good and evil. The article reprinted here was bitterly condemned by the Soviet periodical *Questions of Philosophy*, which compared Kolakowski to "bourgeois thinkers" such as Russell, Dewey and Croce. A short time ago, Kolakowski was appointed editor-in-chief of the new *Journal of Philosophy*, which is to replace the defunct Stalinist publication, *Philosophical Thought*. His "Permanent and Transitory Aspects of Marxism" appeared in *Nowa Kultura* of January 27, 1957.

JAN STRZELECKI, a young sociologist, is considered one of the nation's most promising intellectuals. After the war, he was one of the leaders of a group advocating "humanistic Socialism," and many of his efforts were directed at linking this movement with Polish intellectual traditions. In 1948, the movement was attacked as a dangerous deviation from Marxism and, like all "deviationism," was suppressed. From that time on, Strzelecki gradually withdrew from public activity, and until Gomulka's return to power in October 1956 published nothing in the press. His "Notes" indicate the reasons for his silence and are a good illustration of his thinking, which is deeply influenced by Western, and particularly, French philosophy. "Notes: 1950-1953" appeared in the February 1957 issue of *Tworczosc*.